BUILDING A HOUSE

Mankind is always building. But unless the Lord builds the house, they labour in vain

Sylvia Mary Alison

Foreword by the Revd Sandy Millar

John Hunt
Publishing Limited

First published in 1884 by Marshall Morgan & Scott.
This revised version first published in 2002

Cover illustration: Andrew Milne Design
Typography: Jim Weaver Design

ISBN 1 84298 059 9

Unless otherwise stated, Scripture quotations are from the Authorised
(King James) Version.

Write to:
John Hunt Publishing Ltd
46A West Street
Alresford
Hampshire SO24 9AU
UK

The rights of Sylvia Mary Alison as author of this work have been asserted
in accordance with the Copyright, Designs and Patents Act 1988.

A CIP catalogue record for this book is available from the British Library.

Printed in Guernsey, Channel Islands

Visit us on the Web at: www.johnhunt-publishing.com

Prison Fellowship, England & Wales,
P.O. Box 945, Maldon, Essex CM9 4EW

CONTENTS

Foreword, The Revd Sandy Millar iv
Preface to the first edition vi
Preface to the second edition vii

Part One: Beginnings, 1954 to 1984

1 Learning to listen 2
2 A prophet to the nations 7
3 Living cells 11
4 A new vision 16
5 A child is born 21
6 '... In Jerusalem and in Judaea ...' 26
7 '... to the uttermost part of the earth' 32
8 'til we have built Jerusalem' 38
9 The 'One Body' baby 44
10 Two in one 54
11 The day the rains came 59
12 The work continues 64

Part Two: What happened? 1984 to 2002

13 Co-operating with God 72
14 A sea change 80
15 APAC prisons 87
16 Tracing the threads 96

Endpiece 111
Appendix 1 Letters from Lord Runcie 113
Appendix 2 Reflections on a three-day mission
in Dartmoor prison 114
Appendix 3 How the baby grew and developed 119

FOREWORD

I am delighted to commend for my old friend and parishioner, Sylvia Mary Alison, this new edition of her book *God is Building a House*. It is, as you will see, in two parts: Chapters 1-12 were originally published in 1984, and Chapters 13-16 have been added for this new edition in 2002.

Actually, the roots of her story go back quite a lot earlier than 1984; they really lie in the soil of the first Billy Graham crusade in Britain at Haringey in 1954, where Sylvia Mary committed her life to Christ. It was a new birth for her and began a new calling.

In an extraordinary, yet characteristic way, God has since harnessed the commonplace resources and routines which Sylvia Mary shares with millions of other housewives and mothers, in her case, to promote and participate in some quite revolutionary changes in church and state. So Christian housewives, beware: it could happen to you!

Through an amazing kaleidoscope of people, locations and events, Sylvia Mary recounts the story of how Prison Fellowship in Britain came to birth – an unwanted baby at first to prison officialdom (Prison Fellowship was formally disbarred from entering prisons in its early years) – but one which went on to grow in grace and favour.

Today, an enlightened officialdom not only welcomes Christian lay volunteers in prison, but has sufficient confidence in their usefulness to open whole wings to their ministry. Prison Alpha amongst others is riding high on this sea change in official openness, surfing joyfully over bars and walls to the landfall of hope for prisoners. Sylvia Mary's story of how and where the tide turned – including a little cameo of communication with the late Archbishop Runcie at Buckingham Palace in 1982 – reads like a modern version of the spies at Jericho.

But the story is not just one of a 'baby born' in the world of prison ministry. It is also a story on a much wider canvas appropriately pictured as God the builder. And the building relates to some fundamentally new structures for uniting the dispersed denominations of the Christian church in Britain. The foundations here lie in the Archbishop of Canterbury's venture in faith in launching the 1978 Nationwide initiative in Evangelism. Sylvia Mary was asked to serve on its executive committee, and her story of its eventual breakthrough, from conflict to concord for Catholics and Protestants, features an important historical account of how the late Cardinal Basil Hume led his Catholic flock into participation in 'Churches Together', the successor body to the old British Council of Churches.

Many bricks make a mighty building! But they call for a lot of 'brickies', as Nehemiah found in re-building Jerusalem's wall. Sylvia Mary's story of one such 'bricky' on a bit of the wall, makes great reading and, I feel sure, will inspire many more to take their place in all the many sided aspects of the Kingdom that God is slowly but surely restoring all over the world today.

Sandy Millar
The Reverend Prebendary J A K Millar,
Holy Trinity Brompton
London SW7

PREFACE TO THE FIRST EDITION

Written in 1984

I live with the author of this book. We have been married for twenty-six years. During most of this time she has had to travel on one of the most difficult of all married pilgrimages: that of a parliamentarian's wife. It is no life for a contemplative. She has had to accommodate herself to two homes, one in London, the other in my constituency. Both had to be lived in regularly and actively; and unlike the pleasures involved in possessing second or holiday homes, ceaseless travel between these two bases – often alone but for our young children – involved years of emotional and physical strain. Then she has had to accommodate herself to loneliness. The parliamentarian's working day tends to start at the same time as everybody else's, but to stretch late into the evening. How often has my wife had to sit alone at home, waiting for my late return from the House of Commons, unable to go out on her own account because of the ties of a young family! Then she has had to accommodate herself to endless practical duties of the sort often performed by a husband: driving the car long distances on her own; at home and abroad; organising and supervising repairs and maintenance in the two homes; interviewing headmasters and headmistresses for the children's schooling, and so on – all occasioned by the peculiar demands which parliamentary, and especially ministerial life place upon husbands with full time jobs in Whitehall and Westminster, but with constituencies far away from London.

The glimpse which my wife gives in this book into her inner life and spirit – and more, into that limitless dimension which feeds it – is thus a glimpse into a life stretched outwardly with activity, responsibility and strain. It has not been a life which afforded the time or the inclination for idle fantasies. Although more cerebral than my wife in our shared faith, I can testify that what she writes about is real – for both of us. For my own parliamentary and ministerial life would have been quite impossible, particularly in relation to the occasions of disappointment, strain and illness which affect us all, if the indomitable spirit of faith and hope in her frail body had not provided enough for both of us, and kept the ship afloat.

Michael Alison

PREFACE TO THE SECOND EDITION

part from some minor changes, the first part of this book has been left virtually unchanged since it was first published in 1984. The reader will therefore find reference to events and people that are now changed or deceased.

The second part of the book entitled *Part Two: What Happened: 1984 to 2002* describes, amongst other things, the development of the Prison Fellowship world-wide.

This book is written in the form of a personal testimony. It is basically a call to prayer, a call to Christians to get to know their Lord in a more personal way, and to co-operate with him in his purposes in the world. On the one hand it is a call to closer discipleship and obedience – part of God's preparation of the bride for the Marriage Feast of the Lamb – and on the other hand an attempt to show God at work, as I see it, in renewing and recreating the structures of society according to his holiness and righteousness. It is also about the birth of Prison Fellowship in England and Wales. And it is a book about organic growth, as opposed to organisational structures.

I originally wrote the book because John Hunt, then the Managing Director of Marshall Pickering, asked me to do so. He had heard one or two tapes of talks I had given to Lydia Conferences, and he asked me to write down in book form what I said at meetings. Practically everything in this book I have already spoken out at some meeting or another. Chapters 8, 9, and 11 are taken directly from two tapes spoken at Lydia Conferences in 1981, one in May in Swanick, and one in June in Hove.

I have kept to a certain theme in this book and so naturally have not spoken much about the day to day details of our life. But I am deeply conscious of how much I have failed to be for my children the sort of mother they deserved – each of them so very special, and each deserving far more care and attention than I, with my other preoccupations, ever managed to give them.

There are so many people that I am so grateful to and should thank for so many things, that I don't know where to begin. But I would just like to mention our Monday intercession group, Gwenda Hordern, Audrey Metters, Jane Bretherton, Vivian Sewell (who also typed my manuscript) Jennet Kidd, the late Romany White Abbott, LaDonna Elliott, and an infrequent comer, but very important, Jean Darnall. Together we have learned, week by week, to listen to our Lord, bind up each others hurts and wounds, and worship him. And to know a depth of friendship that is very precious.

Sylvia Mary Alison

PART ONE

BEGINNINGS
1954 TO 1984

To Michael, my beloved husband, and to our children James, Sebastian and Mary Rose, with gratitude for their love and forbearance.

1 LEARNING TO LISTEN

The first time that I became aware of hearing the Holy Spirit speaking was way back in the autumn of 1954. Youth for Christ were holding a series of rallies on Saturday evenings at the Central Hall, Westminster, and on each Saturday they invited two Billy Graham converts to give their testimonies. Billy Graham had held his famous three month crusade at Harringay Arena earlier that year, and in the first week of March I had gone forward at the close of a meeting to commit my life to Christ. That spring I was doing the London Season as a debutante, being presented at court, going to Queen Charlotte's Ball and several of the parties that the Season entailed in those days, and I suppose the rally organisers wanted a contrast in their testimonies, because they asked me to speak with a barrow boy who, as a result of his conversion, was going to be ordained.

My Bible class teacher suggested I pray for a verse of scripture to focus my comments that evening. I had never spoken at a meeting before, and was very nervous. For days I prayed and thought, and the only verse that came to my mind was Acts 1:8: 'But ye shall receive power, after that the Holy Ghost is come upon you: and ye shall be witnesses unto me both in Jerusalem, and Judaea, and Samaria, and unto the uttermost part of the earth.' Baffled, I tried to push the verse away and think of something else. I couldn't. So then I tried to think of something relevant to me that fitted in with the verse. I couldn't think of anything. Finally, I arrived at the Central Hall at the appointed time in a flat panic. I hadn't the faintest idea what I was going to say, and was merely armed with this apparently irrelevant verse which I couldn't think what to do with.

The Central Hall was full. I sat on the platform with what seemed an army of men in dog collars, and the only comforting presence was that of the barrow boy, who appeared to be just as nervous as I was. As the evening went on I became more and more fearful, till the only thing I was conscious of was the loud and painful beating of my heart.

Suddenly, breaking into my panic, came a still small voice. 'Don't be afraid,' the voice said. 'You will be brought before kings and governors for my name's sake. You don't need to think what to say. It will be given you in that hour what you shall speak.'

Calmed and intrigued I listened. What kings? What governors? I was so fascinated by what God was going to do, that I stopped being scared. When it came to my turn to move to the microphone, I was interviewed by one of the clergymen, who asked me questions. Suddenly Acts 1:8 became relevant in answer to one of his questions, so I quoted it. The whole interview can have taken no more than about five minutes. If I'd had a speech prepared I would have had to scrap it, so it's just as well I hadn't. Thankfully I sat down and enjoyed the rest of the evening.

A few days later I received a letter from one of the clergymen. He said that more people had come forward to receive Christ at the end of that meeting than at any other Youth for Christ rally in that series, and it had been through my testimony. Amazed, I stared at the letter. It was awesome. How could anyone have come to Christ through those few disjointed sentences that I couldn't even recall? It was clearly nothing to do with me. 'God's ways are not our ways.'

When I was asked to write this book, I didn't really know at first what it was going to be about. But as I wrote, the main theme that emerged seemed to me to be about learning to listen to God, to recognise the voice of the Holy Spirit.

I would like, in this book, to show you how God has brought to pass the things he showed me that evening when I was eighteen years old, but it was many years before they happened. Jesus says, 'My sheep hear my voice,' and, 'they know my voice'. He calls his disciples not servants, but friends. Friends are people who share secrets with one another. If I try to confide in a friend and that friend doesn't understand me, then I withdraw and talk of more superficial matters. So it is with our Lord. He longs to communicate with his disciples, to share his thoughts with them so that we may co-operate with him in his work in the world.

In the mid 1960s I learned this lesson most vividly. At that time my husband was a member of Parliament, and anyone who knows anything about the life of parliamentarians knows that MPs' wives see very little of their husbands, as the House of Commons sits every afternoon and evening. Throughout the '60s my children were little, and after they went to bed I had many lonely evenings while my husband was out working. I found the loneliness very difficult to take, and would often sink into deep depressions, sometimes lying on my bed and staring at the ceiling for hours, beyond tears. During the day, I'd always had groups of women coming to our flat for Bible study. In the evenings I would often telephone one or other of these women, thinking that I might talk to her and encourage her in her Christian life.

One day, as I was about to pick up the receiver to make such a call, I again sensed the Lord's presence and had a check in my spirit. 'You're not ringing her up to help her, you're ringing her up because you can't bear to be alone.' I paused, considering this thought, and realising that I had been kidding myself. 'But you are not alone: I am with you: I am your husband: talk to me.' I turned away from the telephone, bemused. 'I don't want to be rude, Lord, but I don't think I could talk to you for the whole evening. For half an hour perhaps, but longer than that . . . ?' However, I thought I would try it. I walked back into the sitting room, and sat in a chair pretending that Jesus was in the chair opposite. And then I started, consciously, but silently, to talk to him.

Over a period of time I discovered many things. If you are having a conversation with someone, you shouldn't do all the talking. In order for the conversation to be a dialogue, both people need to talk and listen to each other. Otherwise they won't hear the other's point of view. I soon realised that in my conversations with God I was carrying on a monologue, telling him what I wanted and what I thought about things, but not asking him what he thought. After a time I dried up and couldn't think of anything else to say, so I began to ask him what he thought. Amazingly, new thoughts came into my mind, bits of scripture that I'd never considered before opened up to me. I soon found that for these conversations I needed a Bible beside me to look things up. Another thing I learned was that if you love someone, you don't have to talk, or be talked to, all the time. You can just sit in silence and enjoy each other's company. 'In your presence is fulness of joy, at your right hand there are pleasures for evermore' (Psalm 16:11).

On one occasion, about eight years later, I discovered how much the Lord had taught me. By this time my children were at boarding school, so I was alone during the day as well as in the evenings. One particular week Michael was going to be out every evening except one. I was very excited about that one evening. I bought flowers for the drawing room, his favourite food for supper; I worked all day to make the evening a success. At about six o'clock he telephoned, his voice very disappointed. 'I'm so sorry, something has cropped up. I can't come home after all.' 'It's all right,' I said.

'It doesn't matter at all. I quite understand.' I'd said things like that before, really in order not to discourage Michael, but this time I found that I really meant it. I tried to prod my heart to see what had happened to that depression which would have engulfed me a few years before. But it wasn't there. I spent a very happy evening, in the sitting room with all those lovely flowers, doing nothing in particular, but I kept finding such joy welling up inside me that could hardly contain it, and kept bursting into song. St Paul says: 'Not that I speak in respect of want: for l have learned, in whatever state I am, therewith to be content. I know how to be abased, and I know how to abound; in any and all circumstances I have learned the secret of facing plenty and hunger, abundance and want. 'I can do all things through Christ which strengthens me' (Phil. 4:11-13).

Jesus needs his disciples to be content in him, listening to his voice, and available for him to do what he wants with them: so that when we act we do things not out of our own needs, but in response to his requests and wishes. In this way Jesus, the head of the body, will be able to work through his body on earth.

2 A PROPHET TO THE NATIONS

One day I was walking along the road to our local supermarket to buy groceries for the household. My mind was a jumble of food thoughts. What should we have for supper? What did I need to remember to buy? Quietly, but cutting through all my other thoughts by reaching me at some far deeper level, came again the still small voice. 'I will make you a prophet to the nations.'

I considered this statement with very mixed feelings. Half of me wanted to laugh – it sounded like such a funny idea. I had visions of sprinting round from country to country proclaiming things. Join the jet set! I can't really remember when it was, perhaps 1969 or 1970, but it was at a time when my three children were little. My days consisted of breakfast the school run, shopping, cooking, household chores, tea, supervising homework, supper. . . it hardly left much time for sprinting to Timbuctoo with a message!

On the other hand, this sounded like the Lord speaking, and if God speaks, one dare not laugh. I considered it further. I knew this was a quote from Jeremiah. Was my mind playing tricks on me? Was l just recalling familiar scripture? But why this particular verse? I'd heard of housebound housewives who had fantasies of being film stars. Perhaps this was just a fantasy. Perhaps, rather than producing film star fantasies my subconscious had dredged up the idea that it would be glamorous to be a prophet.

But the message I had heard triggered off other thoughts. A few years previously, in 1966, I'd had a very traumatic day. All day long I'd sensed that a national disaster was impending and would take place the next day. I'd no idea what form the disaster would take. My mind went through every possibility: a nuclear explosion; an invasion; an earthquake; what? I couldn't point to any of these things, but my spirit was deeply troubled, and I paced up and down like a caged animal – waiting.

The next day the Aberfan disaster took place. A coal tip moved and fell on a school, burying alive and wiping out a whole generation of children in a Welsh mining village. The Duke of Edinburgh, representing the monarch, and the Bishop of Llandaff, for the church, went to the scene, thus confirming the accident as a national disaster.

I sat on my bed, stunned. This was what I had been waiting for: I recognised it when it happened. What should I have done? If God impresses something on a person, surely he doesn't do so for fun? Surely it is for that person to act? But act how? I hadn't even prayed; I had simply been agitated. I was terribly sad, grieving for the villagers, and feeling in my immaturity that I had let them down, and let God down. I thought of Moses, who asked God to blot him out, rather than the people in the wilderness, and of St Paul who said he could wish himself cut off from Christ for the sake of his fellow Jews. I had not prayed these things: I had simply not prayed, full stop. What should I have done?

While still wondering, I read my appointed scripture for the day, from the book of Amos. Chapter three, verse seven spoke straight to my heart. 'Surely the Lord God does nothing, without revealing his secret to his servants the prophets (RSV).' It was as if God said to me: I wasn't expecting you to do anything; I was merely informing you of what is happening.

This was the first inkling I'd ever had of being included amongst the prophets. I'd wondered about that verse a great deal. It was an indirect suggestion, but not a direct word. But on this occasion, as I walked along the Earls Court Road, it was a direct word: 'I will make you a prophet to the nations.' My mind also went back to the Central Hall, Westminster. 'Ye shall receive power, after that the Holy Ghost is come upon you, and ye shall be witnesses unto me both in Jerusalem, and Judaea, and in Samaria, and unto the uttermost part of the earth.' Perhaps this witnessing was going to take the form of prophesying to far-flung nations?

My husband is a very sane and sensible man. I felt that if I greeted him with the announcement that God had said that he was going to make me a prophet, Michael would be tempted to look around for the nearest strait-jacket! So finally I said to the Lord, 'Well, Lord, if that's what you want to do, I don't see why you shouldn't. You're God, after all, and you can do what you like, and it's OK by me, as long as you tell me what to say.' After all, if he didn't tell me what to say, then I needn't say anything. That would be easy. And if he wanted me to say something, he would have to tell me what to say, otherwise I shouldn't know what to say. So there was no point in fussing about it. 'Lord, I don't see how you're going to bring this about, but then it's not up to me, it's up to you. You can arrange it how you like. Meanwhile I'm not going to tell anyone about it, in case I'm suffering from *folie de grandeur* and have invented the whole thing. But please, in your own time, confirm it to me, through events or through people quite outside myself to whom I have told nothing.'

I feel really ashamed, recalling this prayer. How rude we are to God, how cavalier! How we take him for granted and order him about! How patient and longsuffering he is with us. He, the King of kings and Lord of lords.

Once, some time ago, he brought to my mind the phrase, 'Jesus is among you as him that serveth.' He was teaching me to be a servant, and he gave me all sorts of boring servant things to do for a few particularly bossy people, in trying circumstances. One day I got utterly fed up. 'Lord,' I said, 'I just *hate* being a servant. I much prefer it when somebody else waits on me than when I wait on somebody else. I do it because you say so, and because you were a servant, and you want your disciples to be servants. But why? What's so special about being a servant? Couldn't you have invented something more fun for your disciples to be?'

Then he answered, something like this: 'If I came to you as King of kings and Lord of lords, you'd be frightened. And if I came to you as one in authority, many people have hangups about those in authority, and would refuse to listen. And if I came to you as your equal, many people have rivalry situations with their equals, and would refuse to listen. But nobody is threatened by a servant. A servant is someone you can order about. You can send him out of the room if you like, you needn't listen to him. He does jobs for you. I am your servant because I love you and out of my love for you I make myself available as your servant, so as not to frighten you off and so that people may be won to my love. That is why I want my disciples to be servants.'

It was embarrassing. The Lord God is my servant. I'm supposed to be his servant, but I'm not. I don't even know how to be a servant. I behave more like a little tin god. One day I shall come before his throne, and find on it my Lord, whom I have spent my life pushing about and ordering around. It will be so shaming. Forgive me, Lord. Please help me to have your heart of a servant.

3 LIVING CELLS

1974 was a very important year for Michael and me. The Conservatives had lost a General Election early that year, and we were searching our hearts and praying to know what God wanted us to do while we were in opposition. Then came a telephone call. 'We want you to come to Washington, to stay in Fellowship House,' came Wallace Haines' familiar voice.

'Who's we?' I asked. 'And what's Fellowship House?'

'Fellowship House is where congressmen and Senators and all sorts of Christians meet for fellowship. And "we" is Billy Graham and Doug Coe.'

As he spoke a paean of praise welled up inside me. I thought I would explode with joy. There also surfaced in my memory those words I had heard in the Central Hall. Could these be the 'kings and governors' God had spoken of twenty years before?

We spent the first week of May in Fellowship House. It was a revelation. Each day we were invited to breakfast with a different group: lawyers, Red Indians, a black group. Michael met with congressmen and senators, and spoke to a group in the Pentagon which included generals. I went to groups in the State Department and the Pentagon, and to a congressional wives group. In all these areas there was a network of cells, groups of Christians meeting in fellowship, sharing ideas and the Scriptures, and praying together. We were twice entertained to dinner in Fellowship House by a cross-section of people belonging to different groups. Here was a living organic growth, members of the body of Christ coming away from their individual cells and merging together in a quite different cluster. I got very excited. There was life and dynamism about these people and they were Christians involved together in their different spheres of work; not simply Christians leading compartmentalised lives – church on Sunday and secular life on weekdays.

I was reminded of a time when I'd been at prayer during my student days in Paris in 1955. It seemed at that time that I was given a glimpse of heaven. The impression I had was of a huge system of cells, like myriads of amoebae, all individuals, but, as they touched each other, becoming one. Jesus was at the centre, but as these amoebae all connected and merged, then he became the whole mass. The connecting fluid that joined them all together, the sap or life blood or whatever, was love. The strength of this love engulfed me and made me weak. It was a stronger sensation than I had ever encountered before, indeed an experience *beyond* sensation. Now in Washington I was seeing some of these cells take on a visible form.

Abraham Vereide, a Norwegian immigrant to the USA earlier this century, was the founder of the work of the Fellowship. A pastor with a gift for personal work, he would walk into congressmen's offices, talk to them about their problems, then pray with them. When he found two or three likeminded people in the same sphere of work, be they business people, lawyers, congressmen, or whatever, he would introduce them to each other and suggest they meet together for prayer and discussion of their common concerns. Soon these little cells started springing up everywhere, meeting for prayer breakfasts. During the time of General Eisenhower's presidency, the group in the Congress and the group in the Senate decided to meet together and invite the President to breakfast. So started the first of the now annual National Prayer Breakfasts, attended by the President.

We have had the privilege of attending three of these

National Breakfasts: the first one of Jimmy Carter's presidency, and two of Ronald Reagan's. At the last one there were nearly 4,000 people from 120 nations. These were mostly people in government, but all were people from little fellowship groups dotted around all over the globe; a network of living cells, black, brown, white, yellow, meeting together in Christ's name.

At that first visit in May of 1974, I was particularly struck by the congressional wives group, to which I was invited as a parliamentary wife. About seventy women met every two weeks in the morning for coffee, to listen to a speaker, to discuss, enjoy fellowship and pray together. I was deeply moved. Since I was eighteen I had been involved in women's Bible study groups, and when Michael entered Parliament in 1964 I had longed for some such group in Parliament, where the wives of MPs of all parties could meet together to pray for the work of Parliament. But however much I tried to do something about it, nothing happened. Now I had a prototype before me. Could not such a thing be done in England? I went home and prayed and thought but still nothing happened.

In the autumn of 1975 Doug Coe passed through London on his way home from a trip to different European countries, and spent the night at our home. Doug succeeded Abraham Vereide, after the latter's death, as leader of the work in Washington, and is a man with a fine, sensitive gift of leadership. During our conversation, which went on late into the night, he made two unconnected comments that stuck in my mind: the first was that he saw me as a hostess in Fellowship work in London; the second was that George Thomas (later Lord Tonypandy), who was soon to become Speaker of the House of Commons, had told him that he would love to see the Speaker's House used in some way for Christian work and fellowship.

It was during 1977 that the project finally took root. In

February that year Michael and I were again in Washington, this time for Jimmy Carter's first Prayer Breakfast. I was again invited to the congressional wives group, this time as the speaker. And it was now that my longing focussed into practical possibility.

On our return to London I went to see the wife of another MP, with whom I had been involved in Bible study in a friend's house. We decided to invite such friends as we thought might be interested from amongst the parliamentary wives to see what might be done, so we sent out postcards and a little group of six of us met all that summer to pray and talk together. From that came the decision to hold a tea party in November that year, and invite a much larger group of parliamentary wives to share with them the idea of forming a group to pray together for the work of Parliament. The question was where to meet? Then I remembered Doug Coe's comment about the Speaker, and we determined to ask him if we might meet in the Speaker's House.

From that time the group has grown. The Parliamentary Wives Christian Group has met every Tuesday while Parliament sits, for discussion, Bible study, prayer and fellowship, since January 1978. Every term we give a dinner with a guest speaker talking about some aspect of Christian life, and to which about eighty people come, men and women from the Houses of Lords and Commons, members of all political parties and all denominations. The wives cook the meal and bring the food. All this takes place in the Speaker's House with Mr Speaker as host.

During the early days of this development, I belonged to another little prayer group. As we prayed we had a picture of the corridors of power, dark and gloomy, and as we prayed it was as if we were opening windows to let the Holy Spirit in to sweep out the gloom with his light. We also had the impression of Jesus saying that he would love to move through the Houses of Parliament, but that he needed us to help him.

'How come you need our help, Lord?' we asked. 'Aren't you God? Can't you do what you like?' The answer came that he didn't want to come in wrath and judgement but that he wanted to come in love. For that he needed his bride, his body, to co-operate with him and show forth his love.

The first three years were very hard going. Each Tuesday a blackness came over me. I struggled with depression and oppression. Once, in our intercession group, I cried out to the Lord and asked him why I so dreaded Tuesdays. I wanted to serve him, but with gladness, not with dread. The answer came that it wasn't much fun for him either in Gethsemane. He endured the cross for the joy that was set before him. It felt as though a great ploughing and churning up of rocky soil was going on through my soul. Then in October of 1981 this changed. I suddenly realised the whole thing felt quite different, as if I were sitting back and watching little seedlings sprout out of the earth. October 1982 felt different again. By this time they had developed into a sturdy little shrub, with growth and vitality and unity.

At Christmas 1981 the leadership of this group passed into the very capable hands of Susie Stanley, and I was able to sit back and be refreshed by the growth of love in the body of Christ in Parliament. Cells began forming and organic growth taking root, so enabling us to try to affect the thinking and atmosphere of Parliament, in order that God might be recognised as sovereign.

It was most exciting in February 1982, to hear the reports of several of our group who had returned from the National Prayer Breakfast in Washington, having experienced for themselves the excitement of these living cells in government throughout the world.

4 A NEW VISION

When I was a child I was very religious, and from the age of ten prayed hard that God would show me what he wanted me to do with my life. When I was seventeen and in my last term at school and still having no idea about my future, I picked up a magazine one day and read an article about crime and prisons in America. I put down the article aware suddenly that this was the work God wanted me to do.

I was really appalled. My father was a diplomat and I had spent my life in foreign capitals, always in embassy circles. I knew nothing whatever of crime and the seamier side of life. I was in turmoil for several days, then after a particularly restless day I knelt to say the Lord's Prayer. At 'Thy will be done' I hesitated, because I knew that saying that meant committing myself to work in prisons, and I was so afraid. Finally I said it, and committed myself, then great peace settled on me and I slept. Two days later I had a letter from a friend who was a novice in a convent. She had asked the nuns to pray for me and that particularly restless day they had offered prayers for me in their chapel services, that I should know what God had for me to do.

The following spring, March 1954, a friend of mine took me to hear Billy Graham at Harringay. I was amazed at the joy of his team; they were 'serving the Lord with gladness', whereas I was wanting to serve him, but with fear and stress. Two verses Billy quoted struck me; one was, 'I am the way, the truth and the life: no man cometh unto the Father, but by me.' I had never seen the point of Jesus before – it was always God I wanted to please. Now I saw that he was the way to

God. And the second verse was, 'Casting all your care upon him; for he careth for you.' I was so relieved that somebody was prepared to take the strain, because I was feeling so stressed. So I went forward at the end of the meeting and asked Christ into my life. And from that time forward the whole emphasis of my commitment changed. It was now no longer that I had to go to prisons and borstals, but rather that Jesus, out of his love for people, wanted to go into the prisons, and he was merely inviting me to go along with him. So the whole thing became an adventure.

I next trained to do social work at the London School of Economics, and then worked in a Salvation Army approved school for girls from fifteen to eighteen years old (a VD treatment school), and then at what later became the Henderson Hospital. At that time it was a social rehabilitation unit for psychopaths run by Dr Maxwell Jones. I was a social therapist, attached to a men's ward of twenty-eight men aged from eighteen to sixty.

I learnt many spiritual lessons there, and among them a very important one that changed my attitude to people greatly. Up until this time I had no conviction of sin. I knew generally that I was a sinner – at least I didn't dare contradict that view – but I had no sense of my own sinfulness, having been a 'goody-goody' all my life, trying hard to obey the law. At the unit the treatment was group therapy, and what happened to me was that time after time while some man or woman in the group was under the spotlight in discussion, the Holy Spirit would shine into the recesses of my heart and show me something in myself similar to the person under discussion. It wasn't long before I realised that there wasn't anything wrong in anyone else that wasn't wrong in me too. It was a most painful experience; I was ill twice and lost a great deal of weight as I became aware of the awfulness of sin, and of my own sinfulness. It changed my attitude, because if you are not conscious of your own sin, you are as I was, like the Pharisee in Luke 18, and you become self-righteous and hard towards sinners. But when you realise what Jesus saved you from, then you are filled with love for others and long to share with them God's forgiveness and love. Jesus said of Mary Magdalene that her love was so great because she had been forgiven so much. The experience also gave me a tiny glimpse of what it was like for Jesus to 'be [made] sin for us, who knew no sin' (2 Cor. 5:21).

In 1958 Michael and I got married and for eighteen years nothing that happened in my life had any connection with the work I had hoped to do in prisons. I often longed to go into a prison, but I couldn't think how to get there, or what I would do if I did get there. So I stayed at home and looked after our three children, wondering what all the training had been for.

Then, in that first visit to Fellowship House in Washington, Michael met Chuck Colson. He had been Special Counsel to President Nixon, had recently become a Christian, and was at that time awaiting trial for offences connected with Watergate. His story is vividly told in his book *Born Again*. Michael met him on a visit to Boston, where they were guests of Tom Phillips, the man through whom Chuck had become a Christian, and they struck up a friendship. Michael wrote to him in prison and, in the summer of 1976, Doug Coe telephoned and asked us if we would have Chuck and his wife and daughter to stay with us in London for two weeks during their European trip. We were delighted to have them, and from then a new adventure started.

While Chuck was staying with us that summer he told us about his plans. He had started a little prayer and Bible discussion fellowship with other prisoners while he was himself in prison, and though he had not yet committed himself to what has since become Prison Fellowship in America, he had started schemes for training and discipling prisoners for Christ. As he spoke my heart started to stir, and all my preparation of twenty years previously came to my mind. However, I said nothing.

The following January, the time of Jimmy Carter's first Prayer Breakfast, we stayed with the Colsons in Washington, and were in Chuck's office on the day when the Federal Head of Prisons gave Chuck permission to go into forty prisons for teaching and training. I shared with the office staff a prophecy that Jean Darnall had brought to us, that God was going to bring revival to the prisons throughout the world and that this was going to be through prisoners sharing Christ with each other.

March 1978 found me travelling in the States with Jean Darnall, and Chuck arranged for me to visit Pleasanton, a women's prison near San Francisco, on the same day as a Prison Fellowship team was going in to conduct a seminar. A few days before this the Lord impressed on me that I would be speaking to these women and he gave me the verse about Jesus from Psalm 22, 'I am a worm, and no man' to talk about. I was very surprised as I hadn't expected to be speaking to them. At a prayer meeting a couple of days before the visit, someone had a picture of these women's hearts, very hard, with iron bars across them. As I spoke these words the bars would open and the women's hearts would be set free. So I was very excited about that. The whole visit – my first time ever in a prison – was an amazing experience for me. I felt so at home there, totally identified with the prisoners and also at one with the visiting team. I felt that I could have spent the rest of my life there. When I was asked to speak, and spoke out the words Jesus gave me, I knew I had perfect communication with the women. And at the end of the evening several of them came to shake my hand, and their faces were shining.

I returned to England bemused, and in April that year

Michael and I went to a Christian conference with Lord Longford. When I was eighteen someone had suggested that if I wanted to work for prisoners I should ring up Lord Longford and ask if I could work for him. However I was much too shy to do any such thing. On this occasion, the first time I had ever met him, we just chatted about Chuck's work in America. But after breakfast the next day he came to me and said: 'I have very strong guidance, and my guidance is that you are going to initiate Prison Fellowship in England.' He didn't know anything at all about me, or my past experience. He went on: 'I thought I was going to do something about it, but God said, "No, you are to stand back. Mrs Alison is going to do it."' 'I was stunned, but equally I recognised the authority of what he said. At last everything was fitting into place.

'Well,' said Lord Longford, 'you're leader. So what shall we do?' Dazed, the only thing I could think of was that verse where Jesus says, 'Where two or three are gathered together in my name, there am I in the midst.' I suggested that we might collect two or three people and pray together, and ask Jesus what he would like to do with us. 'Right,' said Lord Longford. 'Whom shall we have?'

Our first meeting, later in April, consisted of Lord Longford, Michael, Anthony Cordle and me, and took place in an interview room in the House of Lords. We prayed and worshipped together, and agreed to meet again, and next time Anthony invited John Harris and Ross Simpson to join us. Fortnightly throughout the summer of 1978 we met and prayed, and from this emerged a desire to have a conference to which we would invite as many Christians we could find from all over England, and from all denominations, who were already involved with prisons, and we would invite Chuck Colson to share with us how Prison Fellowship started in America and what God was doing through that.

5 A CHILD IS BORN

During that summer, leading up to the '78 November Conference, I received a letter from Chuck Colson saying that he would come and speak to us, but also assuming that we were doing a number of things, none of which we were doing. When I received this letter I caved in, in a feeling of total inadequacy and uselessness. 'What are we supposed to be doing, Lord?' I asked. 'I don't know the first thing about prisons. I haven't the faintest idea what we are supposed to do. In fact we're not doing anything; we're just sitting in a heap, praying. I'm supposed to be leader of this thing and I haven't the least idea where I am leading anybody to.'

Armed with this complaint, I went to our intercession group and wailed at the Lord, 'Lord, help! *What* are we supposed to be *doing*?'

As we prayed, the Lord gave us a picture of a house. It was a very big house and took in the whole of England. Because it was so big the foundations had to be very deep. The ground floor of this house was the prison population and the people that the rest of society have cast off, and then the other floors were all the different sectors of society: at the very top, as a covering to this house, were the Throne and the Crown. The Lord impressed on us that he was shaking up the whole of society, and that we were not to be worried by this shaking; he was rebuilding, from the foundations upward, according to his holiness and righteousness. As we waited on him further he impressed on us the verse from Psalm 127: 'Except the LORD build the house, they labour in vain that build it.' And then, as an added bonus, the further verse from the same Psalm: 'He giveth to his beloved in sleep.' It was as if he were saying, 'Don't worry about it, I'm building this house. You can relax.'

It was amazing. What new adventure was the Lord leading us into? What a breathtaking revelation! As I searched the Scriptures that summer I was drawn to Exodus 35, where Moses calls the people together to build the tabernacle. He calls to the people of willing and generous hearts, to give of their gifts and skills to help build the tabernacle. As I prayed about it, it seemed that we were to call together men and women of generous hearts, Christians of all denominations already involved in the prisons: probation officers, social workers, prison staff, visitors, magistrates, police, solicitors, ex-prisoners, intercessors, businessmen, housewives and share with them what God was doing, and then they would offer their gifts and skills to help build the house. The Lord also impressed on me that he wanted all the prison chaplains involved, because he was collecting his whole body, from all denominations, and the chaplains are the pastors of the flock. With this in mind, I asked the Chaplain-General of Prisons if I might come and see him and talk to him about it.

Early in July 1978 there was a service of thanksgiving in Westminster Abbey for 100 years of the Prison Service. Michael and I were invited, as at that time Michael was an Opposition front-bench spokesman on Home Affairs. All the chaplains, led by the Chaplain-General, processed up the aisle. The address was given by the Catholic Bishop of Middlesborough. I sat there thinking of the things that God had said that he was going to do. As the prisons crumbled, he was going to set up a network of living stones to take care of the prison population.

For many years I still had the habit of reading the verse of Scripture in *The Times* each day, and praying about it. Often the Lord has drawn my attention to something through it.

The day of the Thanksgiving Service at the Abbey happened to be my birthday, so a few days previously I had asked the Lord if he would very kindly give me a verse in The Times, to encourage me, or direct me, as a birthday present. Up till that time I had kept God's word in my heart, or had perhaps shared it with a few like-minded friends, but I had not spoken it out in public. Now the time was coming when I was going to have to speak out what God was going to do. I had an appointment to see the Chaplain-General a few days later, and we were also to hold a meeting in a committee room in the House of Lords in July, to which we had invited seventy people. I was extremely nervous.

That morning found me in a state of great anticipation, running to the front door for the papers, and my birthday verse. It was Luke 1:45: 'Blessed is she that believed: for there shall be a performance of those things which were told her from the Lord.'

God's ways are not our ways.

At the November Conference in Church House, Westminster, 170 people were present. We had a most exciting presentation from Chuck Colson and his aide, Gordon Loux, of the work of Prison Fellowship in America. They put forward all sorts of ideas. The most important of these was the concept of taking a teacher and team of Christians into the prison to hold a week's seminar. Another aspect of their work was to bring out twelve prisoners, two from each of six different prisons, for a two-week training and discipling conference. Then they are sent back to finish their time in prison, but as Christian cell leaders, to share their faith with other prisoners.

The shape the conference should take had been very clear to me, all except the last hour. Who should sum up at the end? What should be done at that time? As I prayed it was impressed on me that I should stand there, and that God would bring forth a baby. Just that. I didn't know what I was going to say, or what anyone else would say. Just that God was going to bring forth a baby.

It was a most painful last hour. I hadn't dared tell the men about this baby so they hadn't the faintest idea what I was going to do. I didn't know myself. We had started well, but as I stood there all sorts of anger and hostility and negative reactions came from all over the floor. There were some people there who had worked in prisons for many years and thought that nothing new could or should be done. The high level of expectancy sank to rock bottom. Everything seemed to disintegrate. I finally sat down and handed the meeting to Michael. He salvaged the situation by calling for a further conference in March 1979.

That weekend was terrible. How could I have been so nutty as to think that I could stand on a platform, and a baby would be born? Was it just pride that had made me take that last hour? Should I have asked one of the men to preside over it? Was I merely trying to assert myself as leader over them? I was very sad. I had clearly let God down. I had misunderstood him, or misheard him. Anyhow, a baby hadn't been born.

On Monday afternoon I weighed myself and found that I had lost seven pounds in weight since Friday evening. I then collapsed with exhaustion and depression and sadness.

On Tuesday I received a lovely letter from Tony Ralls, an ex-prisoner who had been at the conference. 'God wants to encourage you,' he wrote, 'because you have just given birth to a spiritual baby, and you are suffering from post-natal depression. And it doesn't matter about being weak and foolish, because God uses weak things and foolish things.'

God's ways are not our ways.

In March I was able to share this with the second conference that Michael had convened. This little baby would grow up and develop to adulthood as all of us, of all denominations, of all sectors of society, with different gifts and skills and roles and functions, brothers and sisters in Christ, met together and worshipped and prayed for the prisons and prisoners and looked to see what God would have us do. There would be little cells, twos and threes gathered together in Christ's name, little nuclei to which more people could attach themselves, a group in the end for each of the 123 prisons in the country, a core group to take on the responsibility of being the centre of a far larger group. The vision was of cells, birth, a baby, organic growth – as we see in nature; God's ways, not man's structures. The Incarnation, Emmanuel, God with us.

So with the unanimity of the entire group, Prison Christian Fellowship was launched.

In 1985 we changed our name to Prison Fellowship, England & Wales, to fit in with the growing body of countries chartered to Prison Fellowship International.

6 '... IN JERUSALEM AND IN JUDAEA ...'

One of the people who came to that first conference at Church House was the Revd David Jardine, who had a ministry to prisoners in Crumlin Road Prison, Belfast. He told me about some of the wonderful things God was doing amongst the prisoners: men coming to Christ and meeting for fellowship and Bible study; growing as Christians in their little groups; conversions amongst the terrorists both loyalist and republican. The difficulty was when they left prison and went back to their ghettoes: how were they to stand as Christians when they were being urged on to further violence, and punished for failing to obey orders?

My heart went out to this man. I longed to go and be with him in Crumlin Road Prison. However I didn't see how this was to come about.

The following spring, April 1979, there was a general election. Mrs Thatcher became Prime Minister, and in May she appointed Michael as Minister of State for Northern Ireland with, amongst other things, responsibility for the prisons. I had to laugh. God certainly gives one the desires of one's heart!

I felt as if I were on a mission for the King of kings. Each time we flew over in the RAF plane, and stayed in Stormont House or Hillsborough Castle, I prayed that someone would cross my path, someone who would be relevant for Prison Fellowship, Protestant or Catholic. I longed to go into a prison, but Michael wouldn't allow me to until we really understood the situation there. He was also Minister responsible for Health in Northern Ireland, so he said that what would help him was if I went round the mental hospitals and psychiatric units, as I had had relevant experience, as a social worker. I was half reluctant to do this, but felt that if I did my stuff in the mental hospitals, I might be allowed into the prisons as a reward for good behaviour!

But all the time my understanding was being enlarged. God had said that the ground floor of the house he had shown me was the prison population and the people that the rest of society had cast off. I hadn't really taken in who these other people might be. But now as I went round the mental hospitals, it was as if the Holy Spirit was nudging me and saying, 'Look . . . these people are part of my ground floor too.'

Eventually, in February 1980, we went to a service in the chapel of Crumlin Road Prison, with David Jardine preaching. It was a beautiful service. Terrorists who had come to faith in Christ played guitars and sang their testimonies. I was thrilled to be there. It was a communion service and I very much wanted to take communion with the prisoners, but the Governor told us we must leave the chapel before the communion. I was so distressed. I asked Michael if he could go out with the Governor and the detectives, and if I could stay and take communion with the prisoners. Michael said no, we must do as we were told and not make any fuss.

I tore myself away from the chapel with a terrible pain in my heart. I so wanted to stay. When I got home the intensity of that pain was so great that I could do nothing but lie on my bed and weep. 'What's the matter with me, Lord?' I said. 'Why have I got this pain?'

Then God explained it to me, through the verse in Romans 5: '. . . the love of God is shed abroad in our hearts by the Holy Ghost which is given to us.' What he gave me to understand was that he wanted to pour out his love through the prisons, through the very heart of the terrorist situation, in such strength that it would sweep out before it all the fear and intimidation and hatred. But in order to do this, he needed a body through which to express this love. If you love somebody and if you are unable to express this love for some reason, your whole body aches. This was the pain I was feeling, Jesus' pain. This body that he needed had to be not one person, or two or three people, but the whole body of Christ, Catholic and Protestant together, loving one another, sharing fellowship together, a united body through which he could pour his love, the 'perfect love which casts out fear'.

William Fitch, a Belfast accountant and well known in evangelical circles, had invited Chuck Colson to Belfast to speak at a special showing of his film *Born Again*. I asked William if I could possibly borrow a morning out of Chuck's busy schedule, to hold a very private meeting, to which we would invite the forty-five people on my list of Christians involved in prison work in Northern Ireland. William agreed to this, and we held a meeting, to which twenty-seven people came, and Chuck and Gordon Loux talked about Prison Fellowship, and shared this concept of God's love being poured out through one body. Unanimously the people there wanted to start this work in Northern Ireland.

We had one further meeting at which Ross Simpson and I shared with them the concept of a few people of all denominations forming a core group to take on the responsibility for Northern Ireland, and then it was over to them. They set up their own group, their own charitable trust, and appointed a Catholic and a Protestant as co-workers, to go into the prisons together. In 1984, after two years of praying, in one prison the prisoners of both denominations were coming together in fellowship, crossing the divide. In the other prisons it hadn't happened yet. Protestants are coming to Christ in Protestant groups and

Catholics in Catholic groups, but there was still a great divide between them. They need our prayers, that the love of God might draw them together and break down the barriers.

When we held our first conference at Church House, visitors from Scotland had come, asking Chuck Colson to visit Scotland to talk to them about Prison Fellowship. From that time we prayed about how to proceed in Scotland.

By early 1980 we had made a policy decision not to try to run Prison Fellowship in Northern Ireland or in Scotland from London, but rather to go to those countries and find core groups of committed Christians, already involved in the prison service, to take on the responsibility for those countries. In each place the prison administration was different, the network of relationships was different. In order for a movement of the Holy Spirit to change a society, Christian people, in whom dwells God's Spirit, need to be in strategic places within those structures.

In Northern Ireland the opportunity came almost immediately after Prison Fellowship in England and Wales was launched. What about Scotland?

In May 1978 I had been invited to Glasgow to speak at a dinner to launch the Lydia Fellowship in Scotland.

The Lydia Fellowship was started by Shelagh McAlpine. She and Joy Dawson had met to pray and intercede in New Zealand for several years, and when the McAlpines came to England, Shelagh collected together two or three women in Sussex to start praying for this country. This little group grew and multiplied, and soon little groups started springing up all over the country. They called themselves Lydia from the seller of purple in the book of Acts, who was converted through Paul's preaching and opened her home to the Christians.

Then news of a remarkable prophecy reached Shelagh, and greatly encouraged her and all the Lydia movement. In Jerusalem there lived a nun called Mother Barbara. She was a

Romanoff, of the Tsar's family, and in 1911 she had gone to a monastery in Russia to ask the monks to pray for her family who were in danger from the revolutionaries. One of the monks had a prophecy, and his prophecy included many things. One was that Russia would flow with rivers of blood, one that Germany would be cut in two, and one was that Britain would come to the brink of destruction, but would be saved by praying women.

I first met this group when Jeanne Harper, at that time their leader, invited me to speak at their annual conference in 1977, to share about items in Parliament that needed prayer. I asked them to pray for the formation of the Parliamentary Wives Group, which took place that year. The Lydia Fellowship has grown and grown. It was with a Lydia group in Canterbury the following April that we first shared our dreams of a Prison Fellowship. And they gave us our first cheque as seed money for the Fellowship. It was to the Lydias that I wrote when we envisaged a conference in Church House with Chuck as speaker, and they who sent us the names of Christians involved in prisons throughout the country. And whenever we had a prayer request I would ring them up and they would send our requests throughout their prayer chains.

So it was to the Lydias in Scotland that I wrote asking for names of Christians involved in prisons, and we started a list of people in Scotland as we had in Northern Ireland.

In December 1980 I received an invitation from Louise Purvis, the wife of John Purvis, a member of the European Parliament, to come to Scotland the following June to speak about the Parliamentary Wives Group to a Christian women's luncheon club, and also to speak to a Lydia Fellowship prayer group. I felt this was an important invitation that I must accept. All the time we were feeling for an opening for Prison Fellowship. How would this come about? Surely speaking to a group of women wouldn't start Prison Fellowship in Scotland? Still I might meet some relevant person. I accepted the invitation although June '81 was an impossible time for me. We were due to move house that month.

In April '81 Louise telephoned me to make final arrangements. She had read Chuck Colson's *Born Again*, she said, and if there was anything she could do to help Prison Fellowship take off in Scotland, she'd be delighted.

Then the idea struck me. Would she like to ask the people on our list to a meeting? Then I could share with them the vision of Prison Fellowship and they could decide for themselves if they wanted to start it, and invite Chuck Colson to speak to them. She quickly agreed. We had only six weeks. She invited them all to lunch in her home near St Andrews and twenty of the thirty or so people accepted, and travelled from all over Scotland to come to the lunch.

It was a most exciting though stressful week. We moved house on the Monday, and on Tuesday I flew to Edinburgh, to be met by Louise and her comforting hospitality. We had a marvellous lunch meeting on Wednesday with most dedicated men and women, already involved in the prison scene. And at that meeting was the core group that came together to take on the responsibility for Prison Fellowship Scotland. Louise agreed to hers being the address to which people wrote so that there should be one centre for communications, to avoid confusion.

Later that year William Fitch of Northern Ireland was asked to arrange Chuck's visit, which took place in November '81, and then Prison Fellowship Scotland was officially launched.

'Ye shall be witnesses unto me both in Jerusalem, and in Judaea, and in Samaria, and unto the utter most part of the earth.'

7 '... TO THE UTTERMOST PART OF THE EARTH'

In October 1979 Michael and I had a lovely holiday in Canada and New England. We'd gone to stay with friends in Boston, then flew to Canada for a few days before driving slowly back to Boston enjoying the beautiful scenery and changing colours of the New England fall.

We had arrived utterly exhausted. Prison Fellowship England and Wales had been launched in March that year, then in April there had been the General Election. In May Michael was appointed Minister of State in Northern Ireland, and we spent the rest of that summer bouncing back and forth between London and Belfast, like yo-yos. By the autumn we were very weary and flew out to stay with friends and relax.

One Sunday morning we were sitting in church in Toronto, when suddenly it seemed as though the Holy Spirit was starting to impress on me how to set up Prison Fellowship in Canada. My heart sank.

I thought our Lord was asking us to do this while we were there, only another three days! I shrank from the idea of any more work. However the impression grew stronger and clearer, and after a while I became aware that God was also impressing on me how to set up Prison Fellowship in Australia. At this point I became intrigued. Surely he couldn't expect me to do something in Australia while I was in Canada. Perhaps I had better just listen and stop fussing.

Then someone stood up and read the lesson: it was 2 Samuel 7, where David says he would like to build a temple for the Lord. This passage of Scripture broke in on my thoughts; I felt it had something to do with this revelation about Canada and Australia, but I couldn't imagine what.

When Michael and I were together I shared this with him. 'What can this passage mean?' I said. 'What's it got to do with Canada and Australia?'

We read it and Michael pointed out that King David wanted to build a temple for God, but the Lord, speaking through the prophet Nathan, said: not at all, it wasn't David who was going to build a house for God, but God who was going to build a house for David and for his seed, and for ever.

As we read and discussed, another picture filled my mind. This time it was like seeing two photographs, one superimposed on the other. The first 'photograph' was a map of the world, a very interesting and unusual looking map – and although I was most conscious of Canada and Australia, all the countries were there. The second, superimposed, picture was a map of the Kingdom of Heaven. This was triangular in shape: Jesus was the top angle, but somehow he was all of it as well. It was a three-dimensional picture going back and forth in time. People like St Francis of Assisi were there, milling about. It was made up of people, who were taken from every nation of the earth, and it was a body; all the people joining up became different parts of it.

Then the picture shifted and became a building, made up of living stones. Suddenly I realised that the ground floor of this building was the prison population, and the people that the rest of society have cast off; then the different floors were the different sectors of society, ending up with the roof of this building, which was the King of kings, and Lord of lords, seated on his throne. I realised that this was the same house that I had seen in England, only this time I was seeing it world-wide. It was also the same house that God had said he was going to build for King David, and for his seed for ever, and for which the tabernacle, and the temple in the Old Testament were visual aids.

For the next couple of days I felt weak and dazed. I also wondered what I should do with this information about Canada and Australia. Finally I thought, perhaps I should ring Chuck Colson and tell him. Maybe it's his business rather than mine. So on Tuesday evening I rang Chuck, very nervously, at his home in Washington. I thought that he would think I'd flipped! When I got through to him I said: 'In church on Sunday God showed me how to set up Prison Fellowship in Canada and in Australia.' There was a pause, then Chuck said: 'Do you know what I've been doing today?'

'No.'

'I've been in a meeting and we've been trying to work out how to set up Prison Fellowship in Canada and in Australia.'

How wonderful is God! How mighty are his works!

The following year, September 1980, Chuck called together his first Prison Fellowship International Board meeting. It was amazing to think that five years previously Chuck had been in prison himself, and now Prison Fellowship had been launched in USA, England, Northern Ireland, Canada, Australia and New Zealand. And people from sixty-four other countries had written to Washington to make enquiries about setting it up in their countries.

... The ground floor of God's house, worldwide ...

The next time I went to a Board meeting in Washington, the following February, another thing struck me forcefully. I was stunned to see a beautiful map of the world on the wall, in a very fine glass case. What struck me was not so much that it was beautiful and unusually decorated, but that it was the same map that I had seen in the visual image I'd had in Canada. Could I be imagining things, I wondered? I went round the office and looked at a couple of atlases. Perhaps all maps of the world look the same, I thought. But no. The atlas maps were clearly not what I had seen. The map on the wall was.

After the Board meeting I asked Kathryn Grant, the Board's secretary, how the map had got there. She said nobody really knew. Someone had given it to them as a present. Somebody else had appeared, with a skill for glass framing, and had made a frame and put it up. Nobody had authorized it. Suddenly there it was. On this map are little flags to show in what countries Prison Fellowship is forming. It was a breathtaking experience.

In September 1981 Michael and I went abroad again, this time to Australia and New Zealand. Two years previously we'd had a visit in London from the Revd James Worsfold of New Zealand. We discussed Prison Fellowship and he asked us if we would go to New Zealand and share with his colleagues what we were doing in England. I sensed a quickening of the spirit as he spoke. The verse came back to me, '. . . witnesses unto me. . . in all Judaea, Samaria, and unto the uttermost part of the earth'. Surely New Zealand was the uttermost part of the earth from us in England? But how could we possibly envisage making the expensive trip to New Zealand?

The following year again James Worsfold came to England. Again he asked us to come. Again my spirit leaped. So I began to pray in earnest. Later that year Michael decided that we should go out to Australia on business, and should take our next year's annual leave to go. And then, at the February 1981 Prison Fellowship International Board meeting, Chuck asked Peter Blaxall of New Zealand and me to come to the next year's Board meeting with suggestions for our first Triennial Symposium, bringing together people from many countries to pray and think together about those in prison. That clinched it. When we went to Australia that

September we would also go to New Zealand to talk to Peter.

Our three-day visit to New Zealand was wonderful. We arrived in Wellington and attended the Governor's Prayer Breakfast. We were met by Peter Blaxall and entertained by the people who had set up the Prayer Breakfast, who were also the trustees of Prison Fellowship New Zealand. These were a group of people who had attended the Washington Prayer Breakfast in 1978 and had started the movement in New Zealand. Part of the living cells of the body, world-wide.

That evening, as the British High Commissioner was ill, the Assistant High Commissioner gave a reception for us, as Michael, although on a holiday visit, was a Minister in the British Government. To it came several of our new-made friends. Michael had been asked particularly to speak to the Ministry of Justice about Prison Fellowship as he was Minister responsible for prisons in Northern Ireland, and therefore knowledgeable. So we were asked at this reception about Prison Fellowship in England and the value of it to those in prison. Michael spoke extremely well, and then he said, 'But my wife started it in England, and is our chairman, so she should say something about it.' So as I know very little about prisons, I just told them about this house that God is building. I could see the expression on people's faces: they looked very surprised, and very polite. But the acting High Commissioner was wonderful: as he thanked us for our talk, he slammed his fist down on the table and said: 'Isn't it *marvellous*! God is building a house!' And everybody laughed!

The next day we flew to Christchurch. The Mayor of Christchurch, also on the Advisory Council of Prison Fellowship, took us round Paparua Prison, where we met inmates looking forward to the next Saturday's visit from the local Prison Fellowship. That evening he gave a reception for us in his mayor's parlour where we met all the local Prison Fellowship group. Again we were asked to speak.

Earlier that afternoon I had had two hours of deep depression and blackness. I longed to say sensible things about prisons. I envied Michael who, when he speaks, does say sensible things. All I could talk about was this house God was building. In the end I decided that it was no use my trying to say sensible things – if God had wanted somebody sensible he would have picked someone else! So when it came to my turn to speak I again talked about God's house. At the end of the talk a prison officer, sitting next to me, called me over. He was close to tears. Two or three weeks before, as he had been reading the Scriptures in 1 Chronicles, he felt the Holy Spirit impress on him that he was to collect together the vessels to help Solomon build the temple. Only he had no idea what this meant. He and his wife, who was sitting beside him, had prayed together, and had asked the Lord to explain to them what he wanted them to do, as they didn't understand. Now suddenly I appeared from the other end of the world, to explain this picture. Now suddenly he understood what he was supposed to be doing.

We were both in awe, but both encouraged. It is like a jigsaw puzzle, each one of us has his or her own little part to play: if we are obedient to our little bit, the sum of the bits makes up the whole picture. Only God can see the picture on the lid. What a picture! What a house!

8 'TIL WE HAVE BUILT JERUSALEM'

My husband had been a Conservative member of parliament since 1964, first for Barkston Ash in North Yorkshire until 1983, when boundary changes led to the demise of this constituency; and then for Selby (part of the earlier constituency), where he served from the 1983 election until his retirement from parliament in 1997. So politics has been very much the stuff of our lives. And we have lived in both Yorkshire and London.

May 1979 brought in a new Conservative Government with Mrs Thatcher as Prime Minister, and as I prayed about what subject to talk about at the Lydia Annual Conference that month, the following thoughts came to mind.

In March 1966 we had a General Election. Harold Wilson had become Labour Prime Minister in October 1964 after thirteen years of Tory rule, and now after eighteen months he was seeking re-election as he had a very small majority in the House of Commons. One day as I was driving the car in Yorkshire during the election campaign, again the Holy Spirit impressed words on my mind.

'I am bringing judgement on this nation through the Labour Party. Then there will come a period of blessing through the Conservatives.'

I drove on amazed. First I was flabbergasted that the Lord should bother to tell me what he was doing, and secondly, I simply didn't understand it. I am not a very politically minded person, and had I not been married to a politician would probably not take very much interest in politics. I certainly did not think God was a Conservative. Nor Labour.

God is God, and political parties are human institutions, and subject to corruption and decay. Also I knew that there were Christians in the House of Commons in both parties. What could this mean?

It was no surprise, therefore, when Labour won the 1966 election. I told Michael what the Holy Spirit had showed me, and one or two close friends, but mostly I kept it to myself. And I watched to see what would happen, and sought understanding.

As the 1960s went by, the nature of the Labour party changed. At the beginning there were lots of Labour Christians, people such as Methodist ministers, but gradually as time went by they were replaced by an influx of humanists and atheists. By the end of the '60s there was a quite different Labour party. I didn't understand, and I continued to watch and pray, when two things happened in 1978 which began to give me understanding of what God had said in 1966.

One of these things was the visit to this country of President Ceaucescu of Romania. He came over on a State visit, and during his few days in England, was invited to a reception in the Speaker's House. Michael and I were also invited, and as we stood there, the Speaker, George Thomas, brought Mr Ceaucescu and his party round and introduced him to us. I was very amazed by that little encounter and handshake. The thing that struck both Michael and me was that he was grey: he looked grey, his face was grey, his eyes were dead, and he didn't look us in the eye, he looked over our shoulders as he shook hands with us. The sensation was of shaking hands with a block of wood, and the thought that struck us was that this was the opposite of abundant life, it was abundant death.

At that same reception I spoke to various other people who had been trying to entertain Mr Ceaucescu and his

party: the Queen had given a reception at the Palace; a
banquet had been given at the Guildhall for them. The
people I spoke to said it was the most difficult thing in the
world to talk to these guests; they were wooden and
unresponsive. They had tried hard to make them feel happy
and at home, no one discussed politics, but still not a flicker.
One man told me he had sat next to a woman at the
Guildhall who spoke a certain amount of English. If he said
anything quite ordinary like, 'This is nice cabbage', she
would immediately respond by saying, 'We have beautiful
cabbage in the People's Socialist Republic of Romania'. It was
like pressing a button. You got the same response to
everything. Why? Why this response as of dead people?

Later that summer someone sent me a booklet that
suddenly made my thinking fall into place. It was by Richard
Wurmbrand and was called 'Was Karl Marx a Satanist?'
(available from Christian Mission to the Communist World,
PO Box 19, Bromley, BR1 1DJ, England.) It seems pretty clear,
from the letters and writings that he quotes, that indeed
Marx may have been one and therefore it is not surprising
that Marxism, which spread to and overtook so many parts
of the world, should desire to eradicate the worship of and
belief in God. The whole practice of communism is a
counterfeit, a lie from the father of lies – the brotherhood of
man but without a father – a counterfeit of the Christian
family relationship. God is our Father, who sent Christ, his
only Son to die for us, so that we might be born again into his
family through receiving Christ, called in Scripture the first
among many brethren. The concept of equality has been
bedevilled. Of course we are all equal in God's sight, but he
has made each of us unique and special, made in God's
image, with our different gifts and skills and contributions,
and functions, as different from one another as are different
flowers in a garden. God the creator has given us all a

different creativity, a rich profusion, which comes to the full in our life in Christ and Christ in us – 'I am come that they might have life, and that they might have it more abundantly'. The counterfeit of equality has produced the lust for uniformity – same clothes, same houses, same education, sameness, the crushing of creativity. The abundant death that I sensed in Mr Ceacescu's handshake.

Before the 1979 election in Britain, people who were not necessarily Christians were saying, 'If we have a Labour government now, we are going to become like Eastern Europe.' One or two senior Labour politicians were saying, 'We need another proper spell of Labour government, so that we can have full-blooded socialism in this country.'

As we prayed in our little intercession group before the general election that year, we had a sense that God was releasing us from a yoke of bondage as at the time when Moses took the children of Israel out of Egypt and into the Promised Land. That the period of blessing through the Conservatives, God had mentioned in 1966, was about to come. But that it wouldn't be easy. As the time came for the children of Israel to be set free, Pharaoh made their life much more difficult. We had to pray for the Labour party, that it would be set free from Marxist dogma, and that a genuinely viable alternative form of democratic government would emerge from the broken shambles of the Labour party. And we had to pray for the Conservative party, that its leaders would have courage to push through their policies of freeing up the individual from the uniformity of state monopoly. As we prayed for Mrs Thatcher we had a picture of her as a lovely shining jewel, but knew that we needed to pray and intercede for her, as power corrupts and distorts, and the pressures are great, and she needed our constant prayer. It is God who is freeing us from the bondage and giving us new life, not people or parties. And he raises up one and puts down another.

When the people of Israel went into the Promised Land having been taken out of bondage, there was a lot of work for them to do, and they had to get rid of the Hittites and the Amorites and Canaanites and the Jebusites, and the false gods, and clear them up. God wanted them to obey his laws and show forth by their lives and communal living, his holiness and righteousness. They had to clear up the things that were wrong.

We are in a similar situation now. The whole question of sexual morality, marriage, abortion, paedophilia, pornography and homosexuality needs clearing up and laws made that reflect God's holiness. Witchcraft and the occult run riot. Before the Indecent Displays Bill became law we looked in a sex shop window to see what was displayed. I was appalled to see a Black Magic box displayed with a notice about how to fix spells on someone that you lust after. Since 1951 we've had no law to deal with witchcraft, and since then the occult has thrived.

One of the pictures we had as we prayed after the election was of a grey carpet of state control being rolled back over the country and under it, springing up all over the place, small businesses, springing up like flowers. Creativity as opposed to passivity, life instead of death.

A scripture that came to my mind as I prayed about the talk to the Lydia conference that month came from the book of Nehemiah. Nehemiah went back to Jerusalem to rebuild the walls which had been destroyed, and though the enemy mocked the people, they were not discouraged: So we went on rebuilding the wall, and soon it was half its full height, because the people were eager to work . . .

So they all plotted together to come and attack Jerusalem and create confusion, but we prayed to our God and kept men on guard against them day and night . . .

Our enemies thought we would not see them or know

what was happening until they were already upon us, killing us and putting an end to our work. But time after time Jews came to warn us of the plans our enemies were making against us . . .

I saw that the people were worried, so I said to them and to their leaders and officials, 'Don't be afraid of our enemies. Remember how great and terrifying the Lord is, and fight for your fellow-countrymen, your children, your wives and your homes.' Our enemies heard that we had found out what they were plotting, and they realised that God had defeated their plans. Then all of us went back to rebuilding the wall.

From then on half my men worked and half stood guard, wearing coats of armour and armed with spears, shields, and bows. And our leaders gave their full support to the people who were rebuilding the wall. (Nehemiah 4:6, 8-9, 11-12, 14-17, (GNB)

I see the people who are doing the construction as the politicians and business men and those engaged in public life, but the people standing on guard with the spears and shields are the intercessors, protecting the workmen as they build. This means putting on the whole armour of God, and being ready to do spiritual warfare to keep off the enemy while the land is being reconstructed. Will you pray? I still see God as God – not on the side of any political party, but the one who will set the country free from bondage.

9 THE 'ONE BODY' BABY

As well as being involved in politics, Michael has been very involved in church matters all our married life. He was a lay reader in the Church of England in the early years of our marriage, and a member first of the old Church Assembly, then of the General Synod. Although in the early 1960s I was mostly occupied in looking after our three small children, born in 1959, 1961, and 1964, and also with the demands made by living in two places and nursing a constituency, I was, through Michael, made aware of some of the bigger issues involved in the church, and I'd like to share some thoughts and lessons I learned.

In 1966 I went through some painful and difficult experiences in my heart and spirit, which I didn't understand at all at the time, but after it was all over the Holy Spirit explained to me that he had been taking me through the three temptations of Jesus, of course not in the way that Jesus went through them but in a way that made sense to me in my life.

The last of these experiences was very painful. The suggestion made to me was, 'All right, if you want to follow Christ that is fine, but you will come to a nasty sticky end like he did.' That June I was about to give my testimony at a Billy Graham Crusade in Earls Court Arena. I was shortly to be thirty years old. At the Crusade I would be publicly proclaiming my allegiance to Christ. The temptation was to think that when Christ was thirty, he had only three years to live. And the suggestion was that I would be killed through Satanists and black magic people.

For three days and three nights I was really terrified. I would wake in the night pouring sweat – '. . . the terror by night'. During the day I would find it difficult to walk down the passage: my joints felt like water, my bones didn't seem to fit into each other. In the middle of this panic the verse from 2 Timothy 1 came into my mind: 'God hath not given us a spirit of fear; but of power, and of love, and of a sound mind.' I stopped dead in my tracks and thought, there is something funny about all this. When St Stephen was stoned to death he was radiant, he wasn't shaking with fright. Why am I afraid? So I went up to my room and shut the door and said, 'Lord, I don't understand this. I want to follow you, and even if it means that I am going to be killed I still want to follow you. But why the fear?'

When I said that, the fear went away. Then the Holy Spirit showed me that I was being tempted not to follow Christ if the cost was too great. And when I'd understood that, he showed me that during the last few months he had taken me through the three temptations of Jesus.

I was sitting there peacefully in my room enjoying the Lord's presence, when suddenly God spoke. He said: 'I cannot bless the church in this land, because the leaders of the church are not prepared to go the way of the cross.'

This was an enormous surprise to me. I didn't know anything about the church leaders. I didn't know who they were, or what they were up to. But I was very troubled by this remark, because I wondered what would happen to us all if God couldn't bless the church. And it was from this word from God that I thought we must pray, we must see what the Lord wants to do. How can we pray for the church? For church leaders? It was in the second half of the '60s that I got together with a couple of friends, on a weekly basis, to start praying and to seek the Lord's face. At first we prayed for ourselves and our families, but gradually God started to lead us out into bigger prayers for the nation and for the church, at first in our own nation, but gradually world-wide.

That same year, 1966, I was praying for a friend of ours. As I prayed, the Lord impressed on me his grief over this man. Though he was a Christian leader, he was resisting the Holy Spirit in his life. As I continued to pray for him, a strange thing started to happen to me. I started having labour pains and contractions, and feeling as though I were giving birth. I was very puzzled by this, and sought understanding, and two verses of Scripture came to my mind. The first was St Paul saying to the Galatians: 'I travail in birth again until Christ be formed in you,' and the second, a couple of months later, from Hosea 13: 'The pangs of childbirth come for him, but he is an unwise son, for now he does not present himself at the mouth of the womb' (RSV).

Now this second verse of Scripture gave me quite something to think about because when my first child was due to be born, he was lying crooked inside me. It was a very long and difficult birth, because he was heading somewhere where there wasn't an exit. This had made me feel helpless and despairing, because I knew that however much I heaved nothing could possibly happen, as he couldn't get out. This had gone on for what seemed a very long time, until the doctor finally moved him, and then he was born and all was well. But now, several years later, the word, 'an unwise son [who] does not present himself at the mouth of the womb' was confirming my own natural experience, but now in relation to this man for whom I was praying.

At that time there was a man called Edgar Trout who travelled round the country speaking to different Christian groups. He came quite often to our home, and we would pray with him and I would share with him all the things that I didn't understand that were happening to me. When I told him about this word I had had, he said that it was a word of knowledge, and the Lord was saying something to me in a language that I would understand, and that I should keep it in my heart and in his own time the Lord would reveal it.

Well, life went on and I went on praying. I continued to have these labour pains from time to time for fourteen years, but they increased and accelerated and became much more frequent and intense after 1977. During our times of intercession in our group, the Lord would, time and time again, lead us to pray for the church. He would lead us into praying for situations in other countries, and there came a time when he said that he had been asking us to pray just for individual nations, but now he was going to show us things globally. Perhaps we would be praying for Angola, where there was a revolution, but always he would impress on us to pray for the church, pray for the Christians there, pray that people will stand, that they will learn to pray, that they will learn to live in the Spirit.

One day sometime in the late '70s, the Lord led us into a meditation on his body. As we meditated, we were impressed with the fact that a head has one body, not two or three bodies. Shortly after this there was the 500th anniversary of Sir Thomas More's birth, and as part of the celebration there was a service in the Crypt Chapel of the House of Commons. Cardinal Hume, the Catholic Archbishop of Westminster, took this service, and it was the first time a Catholic had taken a service in the Crypt Chapel since the Reformation. The Methodist Lord Tonypandy, then Mr Speaker, was there, as were all the different denominations. But there was such a furore and row about a Catholic taking the service from some members of Parliament, particularly from Northern Ireland. It was so painful and distressing. The truth was being affirmed that Jesus is the head of one body. But what a body! It was such a bad witness to the other MPs who were not Christians, who must have thought that if this was Christianity, who needed it!

One day as we were praying in December 1977, the Lord said, 'Now I am about to take the church through the way of the cross. ' He impressed on us that we were to pray for the Archbishop of Canterbury and the clergy. We started to pray over the next few months, wondering in what way the Lord was going to do this. The next summer, 1978, there was the Lambeth Conference, the conference of Anglican bishops from all over the world. With my limited understanding I thought that as we'd been asked to pray for the Archbishop and clergy, that something dramatic was going to happen at the Lambeth Conference. I thought that if the head of the body (the bishops being the head of the Anglican body) went the way of the cross, the rest of the body would follow too. So we prayed like anything for that conference, and for the bishops. But nothing seemed to get born. And my labour pains went on. Of course later on I realised that I had been thinking only of the Anglican body and not the whole body of Christ.

Meanwhile something else was happening. In January 1978 the Archbishop called together what later became the Nationwide Initiative of Evangelism. This was a group of representatives of all denominations who met to consider how together they could evangelise the country. They formed an executive committee, originally of twelve people. As they wanted some women on it, I was invited as an Anglican, with a Catholic nun, to represent women. We started to meet in March, and we met for a whole day once a month, to pray and worship and discuss together, all different church traditions, to see what the Lord would do, and out of this came the organisation of an assembly at Nottingham in September 1980, to which 900 people came.

Early in that year, Michael and I had a free weekend. It was during our Northern Ireland period, and it was marvellous to have a weekend free of duty. I was most excited at the prospect. But there was to be no peace for me. I spent the entire weekend having labour pains, and I could scarcely sleep at night because of the contractions. So when it came to Monday, and our intercession group meeting, I just lay on the floor and wept. I was exhausted and miserable. 'Lord,' I complained, 'what is going on? I'm utterly fed up with this unwise son. I wish I understood what was going on. If you have an ordinary baby, you know what you are doing. It goes on for nine months and then that's it. And the labour doesn't last very long, just a few hours or maybe a day or two. But this has been going on for fourteen years. How much longer is it going on for? Am I going to be in labour for the next twenty or thirty years? And what is it anyway? I *think* it's a baby, and a disobedient son, but maybe it isn't. Maybe all this is just psychosomatic, and I'm just nuts.'

Then I calmed down and just wept. I said: 'Lord, it doesn't really matter if I do go on in labour for the rest of my life. If you explained it to me I probably wouldn't understand it, so it's not worth your while, I just love you anyway. It *would* be a help though if you could give us a clue about it, even if just to say that I'm nuts.'

Then the Lord gave us two clues. The first was the verses from Romans 8 about the whole creation groaning together for the revealing of the sons of God. And the second was from Isaiah 42 where he says: 'For a long time I have held my peace, I have kept still and restrained myself; now I will cry out like a woman in travail, I will gasp and pant' (verse 14, RSV).

The more I thought about it, the more I thought that this baby was the 'One Body' baby – Jesus as the head of one body – and that it was due to be born during the assembly at Nottingham, when all these different denominations were gathered together.

I arrived at Nottingham feeling completely detached from the whole thing. I thought, one of two things is going to happen here this week. Either people are going to come with contrite hearts, wanting to see what the Lord will do, ready to die to themselves and their preconceived ideas, in which

case a baby will be born. Or else it won't. People will come
with hard hearts, and not want to see what God will do, in
which case the baby will be still-born, or not born at all. In
which case what will happen is that we will be wiped out as
a nation. It will be like Sodom and Gomorrah.

However I expected that it would end in blessing and not
cursing, because a few years previously as we had been
praying, God had said, 'I have heard the prayers of my
people, and I will bless this land.'

From the moment the assembly started on Monday I felt
excited, as one could sense that people really meant business,
and wanted to see what God would do. Then on Friday
morning, before the main speaker, there were two short
items. The first came from the Revd Donald English, a
Methodist and the chairman of the NIE. He gave an
illustration of a human pyramid, in a gym class. There are
four people at the bottom, then another three and then
another two, and finally one at the top. It is essential in order
for the pyramid to work properly, that all the people pull their
weight. If one person slips the whole pyramid collapses. Then
the Revd Tom Houston, a Baptist, who was organising the
assembly, gave a little talk about dying to oneself, which was
essential for us if we were to go forward together.

As these two spoke it was as if the Holy Spirit was giving
me a nudge. I was so excited, and I thought: is this for real?
Am I really seeing what I think I'm seeing? What I think I'm
seeing is the moment of birth: the unity of the body (the
pyramid picture) going through the way of the cross (the
dying bit). This was the head coming through into the
resurrection life.

I happened to be sitting next to a Baptist minister, the Revd
David Pawson, so I asked him what he thought of this. David
was excited, and said this was the prophetic word coming
through for the first time in the NIE. On the other side of me

was sitting a Catholic woman, Vivian Sewell, who is one of our little intercession group in London, and she had come to the conference in order to pray. The previous night she'd been asleep in bed and she woke at 2 a.m. feeling that the Lord was asking her to pray. So she got up and went to the prayer room, where she prayed for one and a half hours. The whole time the focus of her prayers was about dying, and when Tom said his bit about dying, Vivian nudged me and said that that was what the Holy Spirit was wanting to do.

This to me was the most exciting moment. After fourteen years the baby had been born! The wondering and puzzling was over.

That evening we had a talk on the Holy Spirit by Fr Ian Pettit. I had never heard him speak before, but a couple of days previously, as I had been praying for him, I had an impression of his talk as a clear mountain stream, cool and very refreshing, sparkling with lights, a stream of living water. As he spoke that evening his talk was just like that, and we all sat bathed in it. It was the quality of the resurrection life. This talk couldn't have happened earlier in the conference – only after the birth of the baby. It was as if the baby was coming out into the resurrection life, and this quality of life involved the whole body of Christ together, all denominations.

Again, one of our intercessors was praying, and twice God said to him, about the conference: 'You are seeking well, and you are speaking well. Now how about listening?' So I took this message to Donald English, the chairman, and on the Saturday morning he gave a superb address in which he said that we'd been doing a lot of talking, so now how about listening to the Holy Spirit, who might have things to say to us. So he kept us all quiet for ten minutes while we listened.

This is the quality of the resurrection life. In Romans 8:14 we read: 'As many as are led by the Spirit of God, they are the

sons of God.' And Jesus says, 'My sheep hear my voice.' He
wants to communicate with us as we come away from our
preconceived ideas and our old understanding, dying to
ourselves, out into the resurrection life, saying, 'Lord, what
do you want to do? How can we co-operate with you?'

It was a thrilling conference, and I just felt euphoric and
elated. Those who have had babies know that that's how one
sometimes feels after one has given birth to a baby. So now I
thought, either I'm dreaming or this baby has been born.

The following Monday I shared this with our intercession
group, and the Spirit witnessed with all of us that a new
thing had happened, that a new little 'One Body' baby had
been born in England, and was out in the resurrection life.
And we all rejoiced and praised together, 'that a manchild
had been born into the world'.

In 1981 I read an article by Clifford Longley in *The Times*. It
was an assessment of the church, and he quoted the two
dates, 1966 and 1980. He said that in 1966 everything was
going down in terms of numbers: ordinands weren't coming
forward for ordination; numbers were down in theological
colleges; people weren't coming to churches for baptisms
etc. In 1980 there was a whole upturn and now something
different was happening. I was fascinated, because it was
between those two dates that I had experienced my 'labour'.

The month after the Nottingham assembly, as we were
praying, the Lord impressed on us Isaiah 11:1: 'There shall
come forth a shoot from the stump of Jesse, and a branch
shall grow out of his roots' (RSV). We had a picture of a frail
little green shoot coming out of a tree.

Now I had always thought that this referred to Jesus, and
of course it is Jesus in his earthly life, but it is also Jesus in his
resurrection life. The stump is the churches, the structures,
and this little shoot of new life, this frail little thing, is the
new birth that has happened as the different denominations

come to gether to worship. It is the life of Christ coming out of it, and it is the same thing as in Isaiah 53 where it talks about a tender plant coming out of dry ground.

The following March I was in Plymouth speaking to a Lydia Group, and I shared this picture of the baby, and the shoot coming from the stump. After my talk a woman came to me and said: 'In our group we had a picture of a babe in arms, and a stump of a tree with a shoot growing out over a pile of ashes. We didn't know what this picture meant, but there you are explaining the same picture.' It was a lovely confirmation in the Spirit that something was happening.

That evening we had a Prison Fellowship meeting, and just before the meeting a small group of us were praying – the chaplain from Dartmoor prison, a couple of ex-prisoners, a couple of Lydia women and me. The men hadn't been at the afternoon meeting but now one of the ex-prisoners said, 'I've got a picture of a tree, and it's a huge and mighty tree, and it's got masses of branches and masses of leaves, and God came along and he cut off all the branches and all the leaves and he left a stump and out of this stump was growing a new little shoot.' He added, 'I don't know what this means but this is what I'm seeing at the moment.'

And that was what we'd been talking about that afternoon! So it seemed that God was doing a new thing, bringing together people from all over the country, bringing forth the 'One Body' baby as we died to our selves, our preconceived ideas and emerged into the resurrection life: groups of people who wanted to worship God in spirit and in truth, not according to this structure or that structure, or this denomination or that denomination, but following his lead, and listening to him. This new little shoot was the life of Christ in the nation.

10 TWO IN ONE

The body of Christ is made up of different individuals grouped in various denominations, traditions and so on – all those who acknowledge Christ as their head, and want to be his disciples. And one of the most basic human groupings, one of the most significant cells in church life, is the married couple. Their 'one flesh' relationship, the two people as one relationship, is a picture of the community in unity, and of the Godhead itself – three in one.

Once in the early 1960s I was praying for a married couple who were friends of ours. As I prayed, I had a visual impression of a house, looking very nice on the outside. But then the breeze of the Spirit blew and shook the house to its foundations, and as the house shook it could be seen that there were lots of cracks in the walls, all neatly papered over. At about this time there were 'Anglican/Methodist Conversations' going on in church circles. As I considered this picture, relating to our friends' marriage, it was as if the Holy Spirit was saying: 'How can churches unite, and people from different traditions come together, when you don't yet know how to live together in the basic unit, which is marriage?'

In March 1978 I was in California. Jean Darnall was on a preaching tour which took her to many parts of the United States, and she had invited me to accompany her for three weeks as her travelling companion. We had met in St Louis, spent an exciting few days in Oregon, come to Los Angeles for some speaking engagements, and now Jean was in Hawaii leaving me with friends in the Granada Hills.

On this particular March afternoon my friend Mary-Ellen drove me with her on a visit to her doctor, and I was left sitting alone in his waiting room. I sat there contentedly, enjoying the California sunshine, and not thinking of anything in particular, when suddenly I became aware of the Lord God speaking to me. 'I hate divorce,' he said. 'It is an abomination to me when people say "Praise the Lord" and "Hallelujah" and get divorced. It is just as much an abomination to me as when unborn foetuses are killed, and when Jews are put in a gas chamber. Why do you call me "Lord, Lord," and do not the things that I say?'

At the same time as this word, I had a visual impression of husband and wife as one flesh, one entity, and as they got divorced it looked like an amputation, the body was sawn in two and the limbs were left quivering and bleeding. Then as one partner remade his or her life, the other partner was left, cut off from the body, alive still but palpitating and bleeding. Then as I looked, I saw thousands of amputated limbs, all littering the body of Christ, looking rather like those heaps of bodies in photographs of concentration camps, only these heaps were alive and quivering. The Lord of Life was mutilated by divorces.

I sat aghast, with a terrible pain in my heart. The previous year I had spoken at some women's meetings in Washington, New York and Houston, Texas. I had been very grieved, while praying and talking with the women after the meetings, about how many had terrible marriage mix-ups and problems. I thought particularly of one woman who had held my hand and wept. She was struggling with her emotions. Her husband had left her and gone to live with another woman. She was longing to forgive him in order to be able to cope with her own life, but the thought of him sleeping with this other woman was more than she could bear, she was so jealous and bitter and resentful. All I could do was hold on to her and weep with her. Now I saw her as God saw her, an amputated, bleeding limb.

That evening Jean rang me. We were to meet next day at a women's luncheon, at which she was the guest speaker. She asked me if I would say a few words. I asked her what I should speak about. 'Say whatever God gives you to say. He is with you,' she said.

As I brushed my teeth the next morning I said, 'Lord, what would you like me to speak about?' The answer clearly came, 'Tell them what I told you yesterday.'

Jean and I had not compared notes. I did not know the subject of her talk. She spoke on marriage relationships from the life of King David. At the end she introduced me and asked me to speak. I told them what had happened to me the previous afternoon.

Jean later told me that a woman she counselled after the meeting told her she had been contemplating divorce, but was now going to work at putting her marriage together. God's word had acted powerfully on her.

I have belonged to a little intercession group now since 1969. Each week during school term times we have met to fast and pray for the nation. Often we have come with preconceived ideas as to what we wanted to pray for, and each with our different thoughts. But as we have met to acknowledge Christ as Lord, to worship him, to ask for cleansing from our own thoughts and to ask him to show us how to pray, so the Lord has led us into totally unexpected areas of thought. 'Call unto me, and I will answer thee and show thee great and mighty things, which thou knowest not,' says the Lord, through Jeremiah the prophet. Each week has been an adventure. Some weeks it has been very hard work as we have put on the armour of God and united in spiritual warfare against the powers of darkness. Some have been times of deep refreshment and healing of wounds. Sometimes the Scriptures have been revealed to us in a new way, and we've searched them together, our hearts burning within us as the Lord showed us the relevance of his word to the situations we brought before him in prayer.

'My thoughts are not your thoughts, neither are your ways my ways.' Increasingly we have come to say, 'Lord, what do you think? What do you want to do in this situation? How can we help you?'

As we have prayed about marriages over the years: our own, our friends', the divorce laws, the discussion in Synod, he has taught us more and more about his purpose for marriage. Husband and wife are one unit. Through their life together and love for one another children are born. So in Scripture, Christ is called the bridegroom, and the church is the bride. Through the union of Christ and the believer, new birth is brought to the souls of others and more people born into the Kingdom. Marriage on earth is a visual aid to the relationship between our Lord and his bride. It is not surprising that the enemy has been so hard at work attacking and attempting to destroy marriages.

In the autumn of 1979 I was on a train travelling to Exeter in the West Country to speak to a Lydia Fellowship conference. The previous week, while asking for a message for these women, I had been brought to my knees in awe at the thought of God, holy, seated on his throne, and the words that were drawn from me were those of Isaiah: 'Woe is me! for I am undone because I am a man of unclean lips, and I dwell in the midst of a people of unclean lips.' As I pondered this cry, it was borne in on me that I should point to God's thoughts, as being quite different from our thoughts, and show that we were all, in our different ways, stuck in our own thoughts. Our carnal thoughts were like a huge bowl of cold porridge; people got stuck in them preventing them from being able to see God's perspective.

On the train I was thinking of the problem of homosexuality. Earlier that summer I had been walking down the Earls Court Road at closing time, and had been deeply grieved by the sight of so many gays pouring out of the pubs. My heart went out to them in their loneliness and confusion of identity, and I cried out to the Lord, 'What's to be done?' Now that autumn, the Church of England Report on Homosexuality had just been published, and as I read the reports of it in the Christian press, it seemed to me that it was totally stuck in carnal thinking, stuck as in a bowl of cold porridge.

As I prayed and thought and searched the Scriptures on the train my eye was drawn to Luke 16:18: 'Every one who divorces his wife and marries another commits adultery. . .' (RSV). Deeply puzzled I considered this verse. 'What has this got to do with homosexuality, Lord?' Then as I puzzled, I seemed to receive the following understanding. God has made a pattern for mankind, and has given us his word and examples from nature, to teach us. When we ignore his revelation and teaching we make a mess. 'Where there is no vision, the people perish' (Prov. 29:18.) There is no point in tackling the problem of homosexuality until first God's pattern has been looked at. Many heterosexual people have made just as much a mess of their lives as homosexuals. There are many, many people who think that they are married. According to man's carnal thinking, they are. But God doesn't think so: he thinks that they are living in adultery.

11 THE DAY THE RAINS CAME

The United Kingdom is not an island sufficient unto itself: it is part of a much bigger community. It is part of the European Economic Community, and it is also part of an even larger community, that of the Commonwealth, covering a quarter of the world's land mass.

I would like to share with the reader something about the Commonwealth, to ask for your prayers, so that together we can say, 'Lord, how would you like us to help you? How can we co-operate in what you are doing?'

In June 1981 Michael and I were invited by the Prime Minister to attend the Trooping the Colour ceremony from her stand on Horseguards Parade, behind 10 Downing Street. Now this was an enormous honour, and it was quite unlikely that we should have been invited. The reason that we were was that she had invited three widows of the Royal Ulster Constabulary from Fermanagh, with their children. They were women whose husbands had been killed by IRA terrorists, and we were there to escort them, as at that time Michael was a Minister of State in Northern Ireland.

It was the first time I had ever been to the Trooping the Colour ceremony, though I had seen it on TV of course. It was a marvellous sunny day, and when we went in we discovered that all the other guests in Mrs Thatcher's stand were the Commonwealth High Commissioners from all over the world, with their families. The Australian and New Zealand High Commissioners were there, the President of Gambia, and High Commissioners of all the other countries, including the High Commissioner of Uganda whom I'd met before and through whom we'd been able to send vegetable seeds for growing food in the prison compounds in Uganda.

Well, we were sitting there in the sunshine; I had one of
the women from Fermanagh on either side of me; it was the
most superb and exciting thing to watch. The Queen's horse
had been fired on in the Mall, on her way from the Palace, but
we had no hint of that on Horseguards Parade. She arrived
with perfect timing and in complete control, escorted by
Prince Philip, Prince Charles, and the Duke of Kent. The
marching was perfect, the bands of the Coldstream Guards,
the Welsh Guards and the Irish Guards played superbly. As I
sat there my heart was bursting with pride and excitement,
and I thought how marvellous it was. And I could see that
these High Commissioners were all excited too; this was
something we all belonged to: the Monarchy, as the head of
the Commonwealth, world-wide.

As I sat there, I said, 'Lord, why have you given me this treat?
Why am I here?' I felt as if the King of kings, our Lord, had
suddenly scooped me up beside him, and that we were looking
at something together, from his perspective – that I was on the
edge of a revelation. And then I remembered something. And
I thought, Oh, I can't cope with this, it's too big for me.

What I remembered was this. In 1965 Michael and I had
been to a garden party at Buckingham Palace, one of the
three annual parties which the Queen gives, and to which
many people come. We were standing in a line, waiting for
the Queen to come by, when it started to rain. As we stood
there, quietly waiting, I had the impression that the Holy
Spirit was trying to draw my attention to something. At that
time I was learning about the gifts of the Spirit, things like
the laying on of hands for healing, and Edgar Trout had said
to us, 'If the Lord gives you an anointing for something, ask
him, "What is this for?" ' I thought that maybe somebody
was ill and the Lord would like to heal him, so I said, 'Lord,
who is ill? What's this for?' I looked round, and I couldn't see
anybody ill, so I thought that it must be something else, and

asked again, 'Lord, what's it for?' All I could think about was the rain, and the thought shot through my mind that Elijah had asked for it not to rain, and it hadn't rained, and he'd asked for it to rain and it had rained. As I thought this, I heard what sounded like a man's voice saying out loud: 'The prayers of a righteous man availeth much.' I thought it was the man standing next to me who had said it, so I looked at him, but he wasn't saying a thing: he was just staring into space. So I said to the Lord: 'This is very extraordinary, Lord. I don't understand one thing about this. But if you want me to ask for it to stop raining, I'll ask for it to stop raining. So please will you make the rain stop.'

On the word 'stop', the rain stopped. It was as if somebody had switched off a tap. It didn't peter out: it just stopped. Everybody's umbrellas came down. The sky was dark grey, and people were commenting on how odd it was. Why had it stopped raining? Michael turned to me and said, 'How very peculiar. What's happened to the rain? It's stopped.'

I told Michael what had happened. He was so surprised. And so was I. We were both astonished. I hadn't used any faith; I hadn't necessarily believed that God was going to make it stop raining. It had all happened so fast, and almost as a reflex action I had just said, 'Lord, OK, I'll ask; please will you make the rain stop.' So now we agreed together, Michael and I, that I would ask for something specific, and this time exercise faith. It was now 4.40 p.m. and the garden party ended at 6.00 p.m. So I said to the Lord: 'Lord, seeing you've been so very kind as to do this, and seeing you've been so kind as to let me see you doing this, I'd like to ask you something. Please could you stop the rain until 6 o'clock. After six, let it rain as much as you like. But please, no rain till six. Thank you very much.'

So then we walked about the garden having tea and chatting to people. Three different people came up to Michael and said, 'Do you think it's going to rain?' and each time Michael said, 'It will rain after six, but it won't rain before six.' They all looked surprised at his answer to their rhetorical question!

At about 5.50 p.m. we decided to make for our car, so that we'd be in it when the rain came down. So we trotted up Birdcage Walk to the House of Commons where our car was parked. We arrived at 6.05 p.m. just as the rains came down. It simply poured – buckets of water, the sort of rain that jumps six inches off the pavement. As we shut the door of our little car I was shaking with fright. The fear of the Lord fell on me. I didn't dare look up, I was so afraid of God. I sensed his presence everywhere. This is how Noah must have felt when he got into his ark, and the rains came down.

For a long time I puzzled over this. What could this mean? Why had this happened? The more I thought about it over a period of time, the more I thought that this had something to do with the Queen and the Commonwealth. The reason I thought this was because amongst the guests at the garden party were the Commonwealth Prime Ministers, over in London for the Commonwealth Prime Ministers' Conference. I started praying for Rhodesia, which in 1965 had declared UDI. I felt, somehow or other, that God was bringing judgement on the Queen and Commonwealth.

I'd forgotten about this till now. Sixteen years later, here we were at the Trooping the Colour ceremony, and here was this brilliant sunshine, and the Queen and Commonwealth representatives. Prison Fellowship in England had just given vegetable seeds to be planted in the prison grounds in Uganda, for the prisoners to use for food: we felt seeds were a symbol of a new beginning and a new hope. We'd done this through the Ugandan High Commissioner. The Australian High Commissioner was there, and Prison Fellowship in Australia had just started; the New Zealand High Commissioner was there, and we were going to New Zealand in October because Prison Fellowship in New Zealand had just started. I started to shake and to tremble, and it was as if the Lord was impressing on me that he'd brought judgement on the Commonwealth, but now he was going to start building up, from the ground floor up, blessing. 'He will bring forth justice to the nations' (Isaiah 42.1, RSV)

Sometimes one's attention is drawn to something by the way things happen. A couple of weeks after this Trooping the Colour ceremony somebody told me something about a little country called Belize. I had known nothing about this country, but apparently we had not had diplomatic relations with Guatemala for 150 years because of Belize, formerly called British Honduras. It was a tiny little country with a population of 145,000. We were protecting it because the people didn't want to be run by Guatemala, they preferred the British, but there they were in Central America.

The next day, our Prison Fellowship office received a circular letter from the United States saying, amongst other things, that someone in Belize had written asking to start Prison Fellowship there.

The following evening we were at a reception, and were talking to a Foreign Office minister, who started talking about Belize. He said that we were working towards giving it its independence that September, but he was fearful that before this happened there might be troubles, as there often seemed to be troubles as countries became independent.

I thought then that perhaps the Lord would like people to pray for Belize. But perhaps more than that, that he would like us to pray for all the Commonwealth countries. The Lord is doing something mind-blowing and sensational world-wide. This is the impression I had at the Trooping the Colour. Jesus hasn't called us servants. He's called us friends. He's sharing with us his secrets and plans. Will you ask the Lord to show you, personally, how you can pray?

12 THE WORK CONTINUES

One day, during the summer of 1981 I was praying about the direction Prison Fellowship in England should take. We had been going for just over two years and little groups were springing up round the prisons all over the country. I was chairman of the trustees in England, and at that time, as we were still at an embryonic stage, chairman of the little executive group that met monthly to pray for our work and development.

Before our first conference in 1978, as I was walking along a beach in Spain during our summer holiday, the Lord had impressed on me that we should not publicise our work. Before the house could be built, the foundations had to be laid, and this was boring, unglamorous, unphotogenic work. He reminded me of the work of Nehemiah in rebuilding the walls of Jerusalem, and that when the enemy heard about it, they sought to destroy it. So we were to proceed quietly, without publicity.

As if to underline this instruction, during the first two and a half years of our existence, Michael held a ministerial post in Northern Ireland. During this time he had police protection. I was allowed to come and go as I pleased, without detectives, but I was not allowed to publicise my whereabouts. So I spoke to many little groups around the country, without any publicity. The group leaders knew I was coming and arranged meetings. And the people who came to those meetings were a small few who really meant business, those the Lord was calling to pray for people in prison.

But now, as I prayed, I had an impression of all these little groups as a growing army of soldiers, each in their different platoons, with the group leaders as platoon commanders. And I had the thought that what an army needs is a general. And a general needs lieutenants and captains and suchlike, so that between them they can work out a strategy. Because soldiers are not just people milling about; they are disciplined and trained, and can be called into action at a moment's notice.

'That's a great idea, Lord,' I thought. 'But who is this general?' Then came the thought, 'The general is Peter Timms.'

Peter Timms had been Governor of Maidstone Prison, and had been in the prison service for twenty-nine years, as workshop instructor, prison officer, deputy governor and governor. He was the first prison governor to invite me into his prison, and in January 1979 I spent a day with him in Maidstone. The evening before that visit I had been having supper with a girl friend in our kitchen at home. We had, as it were, invited the Lord to join us for supper, and have fellowship with us. I asked him why I was going to Maidstone the next day, and what he would like me to do or learn there. Surprisingly, the Lord impressed on me that I wasn't there to do anything, but that he wanted me to meet a special friend of his, in Peter. 'You're in for a treat,' he said.

As Peter took me round the prison the next day, introducing me to people as we passed them, prison officers and inmates alike, I was carrying on a running commentary in my thoughts to the Lord. 'I see what you mean, Lord. I'm so glad to meet this special friend of yours.'

In April of 1981 Michael and I had gone to lunch with Peter at Maidstone, and had asked him to write a paper for us, working out, through his knowledge of the prison system, how we could take seminars into the prisons, and bring prisoners out for training and discipling classes.

And then that summer Peter left the prison service, was ordained as a Methodist minister, and started work in the East End of London.

Later that year I went to see him and his wife in their new home. I tried very hard to think of something specific to ask him to do. But all I could think of to say in the end was, 'Here is this army, and you are the general.' He responded most surprisingly. 'I'll do anything you want,' he said.

Then he told me that about five years earlier he had woken in the night, and the Lord had impressed on him two things. One was that he was to leave the prison service and be ordained. And secondly, that he was to start a prison prayer fellowship. So in January 1982 Peter became our executive chairman.

All this happened at a time when I felt the restraint on us was being lifted, and we were allowed to start publicising. The little cells were growing and blossoming, with all sorts of creativity, people taking ex-prisoners into their homes, finding them jobs, writing to them, visiting, helping the families of prisoners, all in a grass-roots, low profile, unpublicised way, from the bottom up. Now we needed a more high profile approach.

By March 1984, we had been going for five years. Peter's paper, our Prison Fellowship Development Document, which was written in conjunction with the then Assistant Chaplain-General of Prisons, was sent to every prison chaplain and every prison governor in the country, and also to certain key people in the Home Office, asking for their comments and suggestions. Then it was re-written, to take in the new ideas suggested by different people, and early in 1983 sent out, with a covering letter from the senior chaplains in the Home Office, to all the prison chaplains, prison governors, Prison Fellowship group leaders; to all the bishops, Anglican and Catholic, and the heads of the denominations; and to all the principals of the theological colleges in the country.

Since that time much work began to be done through training weekends, and regional conferences. Peter collected a team called the National Leadership Group, and between them they produced national guidelines for groups, seminars, training of volunteer teams, residential aftercare, finance, and many other aspects of the work. In 1984 we started seminars in the prisons and were enormously helped by having on our team a lovely young woman, Rita Nightingale, who spent three years of a twenty year prison sentence, for alleged drug smuggling in Thailand. Rita became a Christian while in prison, and was visited there by Kathryn Grant, of Prison Fellowship International. On being pardoned and set free she returned to England, and in 1981 became a member of our staff. Her book *Freed for Life*, published in 1982, has been a best seller, and she has told her story of God's grace to many inmates, in many prisons, up and down the British Isles and in the United States.

In July 1983, Chuck Colson held a Prison Fellowship International Symposium. Fifteen chartered countries were present, as were also representatives from seven other countries. The fellowship was deep and immediate. We were one family: black, white, yellow, brown, men and women of different denominations and church traditions, yet one in Christ, seeking to build up the body of Christ in the prison situation.

Looking through the Prison Fellowship Directory for 1984 one can see that of the fifteen chartered countries, eight of them are from the Commonwealth, and of the nine countries that are in the process of being chartered, six of them are Commonwealth countries.

The following is taken from *Notes on the Commonwealth* which I found in the Commonwealth Institute in London:

'The Commonwealth, unlike the United Nations, has no charter. It has, instead, a series of declarations to which all member countries voluntarily subscribe'.

The Declaration of Commonwealth Principles says:

> The Commonwealth of Nations is a voluntary association of independent sovereign states, each responsible for its own policies, consulting and co-operating in the common interests of their peoples and in the promotion of international understanding and world peace ...
>
> We believe that international peace and order are~ essential to the security and prosperity of mankind ...
>
> We believe in the liberty of the individual, in equal rights for all citizens ...
>
> We recognise racial prejudice as a dangerous sickness ...
>
> We oppose all forms of colonial domination and racial oppression and are committed to the principles of human dignity and equality ...
>
> We believe that the wide disparities in wealth now existing between different sections of mankind are too great to be tolerated ...
>
> We believe that international co-operation is essential to remove the causes of war ...
>
> In pursuing these principles the members of the Commonwealth believe that they can provide a constructive example of the multi-national approach which is vital to peace and progress in the modern world. The association is based on consultation, discussion and co-operation ...

The Commonwealth consisted at this time of forty-nine nations and made up a quarter of the world's population. It is a voluntary association and ideally is a reflection to us, in the secular world, of the interrelation between members of the body of Christ, world-wide. It is, however, no more than a reflection, and is made up of 'the kingdoms of this world' with, amongst other things many different religions.

The body of Christ, however, is taken from out of the kingdoms of this world and is made up of those who are disciples of Jesus Christ, the King of kings and Lord of lords.

For the Holy Spirit to change the structures of society, and to build God's house according to God's holiness and righteousness, Christians need to come together to pray and ask God what he would have them to do to co-operate with him. And we need to work within the structures. The Commonwealth is influenced by parliamentary democracy, common law, the Anglican Church and the English language. Latin American countries are influenced by Spanish and Portuguese culture and language, Roman Catholicism, Roman law. These links need to be taken into account when praying for revival and renewal and change. God the Holy Spirit is always at work renewing life.

In our praying, he showed us that the ground floor was the prison population and the people that the rest of society has cast off. Later he showed us that the next layer was the law. In England, groups of magistrates meet to pray, to see what God will show them. This is chiefly to do with the sentencing of offenders, but it is also to do with implementing God's justice. This is God's house that he is building. It has to be built according to his pattern and plan, with both men and women doing their part.

When I was invited to join the Executive Committee of the Nationwide Initiative of Evangelism I asked the Lord if he really meant me to do this. I didn't see myself as a committee person, and couldn't understand what would be the point of my going on it. The Lord gave me to understand something

like this: the men are the head of the body, and the women
the heart. A body doesn't operate properly if it is all head and
no heart, nor if it is all heart and no head. Both are needed.
Men and women have different functions, and different ways
of apprehending truth, but both are needed.

A word to intercessors. Once, in the 1960s, I was deeply
depressed, longing and aching for a ministry, feeling that life
was passing me by and I was achieving nothing. Then one
night, as I was just dropping off to sleep, quietly the Holy
Spirit impressed on me a gentle word: 'When I was in prison
you came to me.' I was totally surprised. Although this word
came as balm to my spirit, encouraging me and making me
feel less forlorn, I was conscious that I had never been inside
a prison. So I said, 'Lord, when did I visit you in prison?' I
reached for my Bible and looked up Matthew 25, and read,
'Then shall the righteous answer ... when saw we thee ... in
prison, and came unto thee?' Even more baffled and
surprised I put down the Bible, feeling strangely comforted,
but not understanding it at all. It was several years before I
ever set foot in a prison.

Of course in our prayer imagination, we can enter any
prison in the world, and visit Christ in the prisoners there.
We have that verse, Matthew 25:36, on all our Prison
Fellowship literature, to remind and encourage ourselves
that it is Christ who beckons us into the darkest of the
world's jails.

Will you co-operate with our Lord in building his house,
from the ground floor up, by marching into every prison of
the world in prayer?

PART TWO

WHAT HAPPENED?
1985 TO 2001

For our lovely granddaughters,
Natasha, Lucy, Daisy and Sophia

13 CO-OPERATING WITH GOD

In 1999 I was asked to be the speaker at the Yorkshire Prayer Breakfast held in May each year. Michael had been the speaker at the first Yorkshire breakfast, held ten years previously, and now, two years after his retirement from Parliament, the organising committee had invited me to speak. I was filled with gladness at the prospect and over the next days and weeks, as I waited on the Lord for something to speak about, the words that kept going through my mind were: Eye has not seen, nor ear heard, nor the heart of man conceived, what God has prepared for those who love him' (1 Cor. 2:9, RSV).

'How lovely, Lord!' I thought. 'But how do I talk about this?'

And as I waited on him further, another scripture kept coming to mind: 'Then I said, 'Lo, I come . . . I delight to do thy will, O my God; thy law is within my heart' (Psalm 40: 7-8, RSV).

This is, of course, about Jesus: first in Psalm 40, and then expounded in Hebrews 10. Putting the two passages together, we have: "Sacrifice and offering thou dost not desire; but thou hast given me an open ear. A body hast thou prepared for me. Then I said, 'Lo, I come; in the roll of the book it is written of me; I delight to do thy will, O my God, thy law is within my heart.'"

As I considered these verses, I thought how beautifully they described Jesus. He came to earth as a man to do his Father's will. He did it willingly, and with joy. He always did what the Father told him to do. He listened to the Father, and spoke not on his own authority but on the Father's authority.

72

He did always those things that pleased him. The word of God was fleshed out in human form in the person of Jesus, who lived on earth as a man two thousand years ago.

But as I considered this further, I thought that those of us, of whatever denomination, who are his followers, his disciples on earth, are his body on earth, as we receive him into our lives and are born anew into his family. And Jesus told his followers, 'Where two or three are gathered together in my name, there am I in the midst of them' (Matt. 18:20). God dwells in the midst of his people.

And as I considered this further still, I thought that the body of Christ is also called the bride of Christ. And we, his bride, need to get to know our Bridegroom, and co-operate with him in his plans for the world.

My mind went back and I thought of what God had taught us in our little Monday intercession group as we had met to pray week by week during the last thirty or so years. Out of our prayers together had come the formation of the Parliamentary Wives Christian Fellowship, and Prison Fellowship in England and Wales. I remembered the picture that God had given us at the start of the wives' group, which I wrote about in chapter 3. Jesus wanted to move through the Houses of Parliament, but he needed our help. He wanted to come in love, and for that he needed his bride, his body, to co-operate with him and show forth his love.

The wives' group, started in 1977, still meets every Tuesday in the Speaker's House while Parliament is sitting. We study the Scriptures together, pray for one another and our husbands, and three times a year we have a dinner party in the Speaker's House, often with Mr Speaker as host, to which we invite members of Parliament, from the Lords and Commons, and their wives. Our little group brings all the food and drink, and we each arrive early, carrying dishes, and laying out the table. And to each of these evenings we invite someone to speak, so that together we might learn about God's ways. Billy Graham came twice, Luis Palau came, as did David Watson, Jackie Pullinger, and countless excellent speakers from different denominations and traditions, both to teach in small groups, or to speak at the dinner, or both. Key speakers from the Catholic Church were Cardinal Basil Hume and Fr Ian Pettit.

As a result of these dinners, people have come to faith in Christ, and we have been strengthened and encouraged. In the mid '90s we even had an Alpha Course (a Christian evangelistic and discipleship training course) for the women, led by members of Holy Trinity Church, Brompton. And the fellowship grew and developed, with regular Bible study meetings amongst the members of Parliament, Lords and Commons, and amongst the staff there.

In the early '80s a small group of people who had been to the Presidential Prayer Breakfast in Washington met together to try to set up such a prayer breakfast in London. Three of us were parliamentary wives who had grown in confidence in what God was doing amongst us. We had that first Prayer Breakfast, which we called the London Prayer Breakfast, in the Savoy Hotel ballroom! By the following year members of Parliament had been drawn in, and three MPs – one Conservative, one Labour and one Liberal – became part of the organising committee, and it became the National Prayer Breakfast, hosted by the then Speaker, George Thomas. This Breakfast has been held every year since that time, and takes place in the Queen Elizabeth II Conference Centre in Parliament Square.

Many people pray for these breakfast meetings, and one day, as a group of us were praying together in St Michael's, Chester Square, just before the second Breakfast – that is, the first National Prayer Breakfast – one of our number was given a picture of a very large fortress, covering the British Isles. It had watchtowers and battlements, with soldiers walking along the battlements and regrouping in the watchtowers. A watchman's job is to keep watch for any signs of an enemy, and to alert the soldiers who are there to protect the people inside the fort. And, of course, intercessors are called watchmen. Somebody said she had seen twelve watchtowers for this large fortress. We understood each watchtower to be a Prayer Breakfast covering a designated part of the country.

When in 1999 I was asked to speak at the Yorkshire Prayer Breakfast, I remembered this picture. So I asked Anthony Cordle, who was part of the organising committee for the first London Breakfast and who has been instrumental in helping set up Prayer Breakfasts in many parts of the UK and also in Commonwealth countries, and in Europe, if he could give me a list of the Breakfasts in the British Isles. I have the list before me:

Regional	National Prayer Breakfast, London
	Prayer Breakfast, Scotland
	Prayer Breakfast, Wales
	United Prayer Breakfast in Ireland, North and South
County	Yorkshire (the first of the counties to have one)
	Shropshire (held its first Breakfast on the morning I was speaking in Yorkshire)
	Kent
	East Sussex
	Cumbria /Lake District
	Inverness/ Highland Prayer Breakfast
City/town	City of London
	Manchester
	Birmingham
	Arbroath

This makes fourteen turrets or watchtowers.

Many people are invited to these Breakfasts, which are each organised by local Christians who meet for fellowship in their communities. Each includes a message from Parliament by an MP or MP's wife. Various people are invited to outline and pray for different needs. There are hymns, and a speaker, and of course a delicious breakfast! There are also seminars to inform people of various local needs and to share vision. On the day I spoke in Yorkshire the 'Prayers' were:

for the nation: Michael Alison
for Yorkshire: Neville Knox
for farming and agriculture: Jim Wilkinson
for ministry to prisons: Oliver Smith.

Neville Knox and Jim Wilkinson are well known Yorkshire figures, and as they prayed I became very aware that they were praying for the bit of land inside the fortress that was Yorkshire. And since 1983 Oliver Smith, also a Yorkshireman, has been a wonderful trustee for Prison Fellowship.

After the interval, the seminar was led by Geoff Ogden (co-ordinator of the East Riding Drug Action Team), assisted by PC David Davies, and they warned us of what was increasingly happening in the Yorkshire villages. This is just what watchmen are supposed to do: alert people of the enemy invading their territory!

In April 2001, as I was considering what the theme of the second part of this book might be, what came to me so clearly was the vision I had in Canada in 1979 of the body and the house, which I wrote about in Chapter 7. The vision was of a map of the Kingdom of Heaven superimposed on a map of all the countries of the world. The map of the Kingdom of Heaven was triangular in shape. Jesus was the top angle, but somehow he was all of the map as well. It was a three-dimensional picture, going back and forth in time, and was full of people taken from all the nations of the earth. All these people started moving about, and they came together in the shape of a man – the body of Christ.

Then the picture changed and all these people started moving again, coming together in a different pattern, and as I watched I saw that they were becoming the shape of a house.

This house built itself up, and I saw that it was the same house that I had seen in England the year before, only now I was seeing it world-wide. The ground floor was the prison population and the people cast off by the rest of society, and the upper floors were the different sectors of society, ending up with the Throne and Crown as the roof of the house. But whereas I had seen our English monarch as the covering to this house, now that I was seeing it world-wide, I saw that it was the King of kings and Lord of lords who was the covering, and that our English monarch had been a visual aid. This was the house that, according to 2 Samuel 7, God had said he was going to build, a house that he would establish for David and his seed, Jesus, and forever-us, for which the temple and the tabernacle had been visual aids. God dwelling in the midst of his people.

As I have been considering all that happened in the last two decades of the last century, I have seen that it is the body of Christ that has been building itself into the house. The prophet Isaiah wrote:

Here is my servant, whom I uphold,
    my chosen one in whom I delight;
I will put my Spirit on him
    and he will bring justice to the nations.
He will not shout or cry out,
    or raise his voice in the streets.
A bruised reed he will not break,

and a smouldering wick he will not snuff out.
In faithfulness he will bring forth justice;
    he will not falter or be discouraged
till he establishes justice on earth.
    In his law the islands will put their hope.

Isaiah 42:1-4, NIV

This passage is, of course, about Israel, about Jesus and about the body of Christ on earth since his resurrection. It is the character of Jesus. He has a work to do, to bring justice to the nations. The bruised reed of verse 3 is the logo of Prison Fellowship. It signifies the kindness and gentleness and love of God to the powerless and broken in the prisons, part of the ground floor of the house. Quietly and faithfully, he will bring forth justice: 'He will not falter or be discouraged till he establishes justice on earth.'

I, the LORD, have called you in righteousness;
    I will take hold of your hand.
I will keep you and will make you
    to be a covenant for the people
    and a light for the Gentiles,
to open eyes that are blind,
    to free captives from prison
and to release from the dungeon
    those who sit in darkness.
I am the LORD; that is my name!
    I will not give my glory to another
    or my praise to idols.
See, the former things have taken place,
    and new things I declare;
before they spring into being
    I announce them to you.

Isaiah 42:6-9, NIV

Prison Fellowship International had its first board meeting in September 1980, and after that met once a year, with executive committee meetings in between. Our first convocation, held in Belfast in 1983, brought together representatives of about thirteen countries. Other convocations followed – in 1986 in Nairobi, Kenya; in 1989 in Costa Rica; in 1992 in Seoul, S. Korea; in 1995 in Washington DC. And in 1999 delegates from eighty-eight countries chartered to Prison Fellowship International met together in Sofia, Bulgaria, for the, up to now, biggest gathering that we've had in one place, at one time. About 110 nations had representatives there. There were Orthodox priests, Catholic priests, clergy of many Protestant denominations, ex-prisoners, volunteers, justice officials, Prison Fellowship staff, and trustees from all the different countries.

At each convocation we spend a week together, worshipping the Lord, having fun and fellowship together, and holding meetings, celebrations and seminars, with regional meetings to express our different concerns in the various regions. The body of Christ, concerned to build the ground floor of God's house, as he leads us: it is a wonderful and awesome experience.

So many amazing initiatives have been taken in so many different countries to help men and women in prison. And as we hear of each other's initiatives, we put them into action in our own countries, as we are able, praising God for all he is doing. And the most exciting of these initiatives is the APAC prison, started in Brazil in 1975.

As we were praying at the beginning stages of trying to set up such a prison in England, the scripture that kept going through my mind was: "The kingdoms of this world will become the kingdom of our Lord and of His Christ". (Revelation 11:15).

In September 2001, at the Council meeting in South Africa there were 95 chartered countries

14 A SEA CHANGE

In the autumn of 1978, before we had our first Prison Fellowship conference, I spent two days feeling completely weak. 'What's the matter with me, Lord?' I asked. 'Why do I feel like this?'

The answer came that the body of Christ in the prisons was terribly weak. There was life in it still, but the pulse was faint. The body had no strength. I was stunned.

'Is there anything we can do to help you, Lord?' I asked.

The Lord showed me that we should worship him. I was to worship him myself, and to lead people in worship, because by doing so we would enter God's throne room and see things from God's point of view: 'With man this is impossible, but with God all things are possible' (Matt. 19:26, NIV). So all our meetings start with worship.

In the summer of 1979, after Prison Fellowship was officially launched, the Chaplain-General invited Michael and me to the chaplains' conference. We were honoured to be invited. Michael flew over from Northern Ireland in a helicopter and arrived in Cambridge with his detective. I came separately. We were invited to dinner and to spend the night and to speak the next morning about Prison Fellowship.

I was very nervous. At the March 1979 conference, when we were launched as an organisation, the chaplains had told us that we could be established as an organisation, and we could pray for the chaplains, but we could not go into the prisons. Then the Chaplain-General had sent a letter to all the chaplains, with a copy to us, telling them they could not let any of us into the prisons until further notice.

A young chaplain greeted us when we arrived at the conference. He told me to take courage and not be afraid because the chaplains were much more afraid of us than we were of them. I asked him why. 'Well, we are very institutionalised,' he said.

We had a lovely evening, with an amusing after dinner speaker who made us all laugh. Then the next morning Michael and I were asked to say a few words. When it came to my turn, I told them about a meeting we had had the previous week at All Souls' Church, Langham Place, with seven of our Prison Fellowship volunteer prayer groups, each group praying for one of the seven London prisons. I had been in the Holloway group which had also included the chaplain; a young deputy governor, a lovely girl with a real heart for prisoners, but very isolated and alone in her Christian walk; and two nuns from a convent near the prison who had prayed for prisoners for many years but had never been inside a prison. As a result of this meeting and time of prayer together, the deputy governor had invited the two nuns to come into the prison and pray with her once a week. I ended by saying, 'It was just a little thing, but it was a building up of the body of Christ thing.'

We were very kindly and courteously received by the chaplains, but I went away with the impression that they were very timid, and I saw what the young chaplain had meant by 'institutionalised'.

A few months later God seemed to speak very clearly. We were at our church, Holy Trinity, Brompton, and the preacher that morning was Bishop Festo Kivengere of Uganda. In February 1977 the much-loved Archbishop Janani Luwum of Uganda had been murdered by Idi Amin, and there had followed a great persecution of the Christians. Festo preached very movingly on the lesson for that day, Ezekiel 34:1-16, about the good and bad shepherds and the sheep. As he spoke, it was as if God was pointing Festo out to me and saying that he was an example of the good shepherd, but in comparison, where was the English prison chaplaincy? I was aghast and cried throughout the rest of the service.

I went home and prayed and cried and asked the Lord, 'What's to be done?' He had impressed on me that he wanted the whole body of Christ, all the denominations, to work together in support of the chaplains, who were the pastors of the flock. They were responsible for the spiritual work in the prisons, but they did things very much on their own, and no outsider could do anything without their permission. As I waited on the Lord, I had an impression of an old dungeon, very dark and gloomy, with little slits high up in the walls, covered over by dirty glass and cobwebs. The chaplains were all sitting isolated in this gloom and they had got used to seeing in this dim light. When we had our first conference in 1978, it was as if we'd opened some of those windows and light and air had come in, which was why they'd been so disturbed – they had been blinking in this unexpected draught and light.

From the beginning, God had shown us that the house that he was building was very big, and therefore the foundations had to be deep, and they had to be based on prayer. The chaplains had said that we could not go into the prisons, but we could pray for them. So we had been happy to start prayer groups, and by the end of the first eighteen months we had groups for 44 of the then 127 prisons. So the chaplains' decree had been a prophetic word to us!

Some years later the Lord impressed on me that when the foundations had been laid, I could stop being Chairman of the Trustees and I stopped in September 1989, when we had approximately a group for each prison.[1]

1 The number of prisons changes as new prisons are built, and old ones closed down.

During these eleven years there were three Chaplain-Generals and we had three Prison Fellowship Directors. Three times a year the Director and I went to the Home Office for a meeting with the senior chaplaincy team. For the first four years we talked and discussed, but they always ended up by saying we could go on praying, but could not enter the prisons. The Lord impressed on us that we were to love the chaplains and pray for them, and be servants to them, and that he would change them.

The second Chaplain-General was very friendly towards us, and liked what we were doing (as well as praying, we were working with ex-prisoners and families of prisoners) but he still refused permission. During this time Michael was a government minister, first in Northern Ireland and then in the Department of Employment. We decided not to go over anybody's head, but to wait for God to open a way.

In the summer of 1982 we were invited to one of the Queen's garden parties in Buckingham Palace. It was a lovely day, and as we strolled round the garden we saw the then Archbishop of Canterbury, Lord Runcie, standing on his own and went over to talk to him. I had heard him speak at the Nationwide Initiative of Evangelism conference in September 1980, but had never met him. When we had greeted him, he turned to me and said, 'What are we going to do about these prison chaplains?' We were astonished.

The Archbishop said he was shortly to be escorted round Maidstone Prison by the Chaplain-General and before that he wanted to talk to our then Director, Peter Timms, who had been Governor of Maidstone Prison. So he asked me if Peter and I would make an appointment to see him at Lambeth Palace.

We had invited the Chaplain-General to lunch, and he came not long before our meeting at Lambeth Palace. He told us that he wanted to write to all the chaplains and tell them that those who wanted to could work with us, but those who did not, need not. We were thrilled with this as the Lord had said he wanted 'men and women of willing hearts to help build his house'. We also knew that there were several chaplains who would love the help of volunteers, and would willingly use us if they were allowed to.

We told the Chaplain-General that we were going to see the Archbishop, and he was very distressed as he thought we were going to complain about the chaplains. We said, 'No, we didn't ask to see the Archbishop, the Archbishop asked to see us.'

When Peter Timms and I arrived at Lambeth Palace, we didn't need to say anything about the chaplains, because the Archbishop was very well briefed. He had been very troubled when the time had come to appoint a new Chaplain-General of Prisons because the chaplains had threatened to go on strike if someone from outside were brought in. 'What does this say about the Church?' he said. As we left he asked me if I wanted him to say anything to the Chaplain-General. I said that it would be lovely if he could affirm and encourage the Chaplain-General's idea of writing to the chaplains saying that those who wanted to could use us. It was his idea and he wanted to do it, but it was being resisted by some senior chaplains, and he needed encouragement from someone in authority over him. The Archbishop was delighted. He said it was the easiest job anyone had ever given him to do.

Later that year the letter went out, and from that time we were able to go into prisons.

In 1988 the next Chaplain-General (who had been brought in from outside the prison service) wrote an open letter to the chaplains in their magazine *New Life*. He had been to our first national weekend conference in 1987, and had loved it. He wrote saying that Prison Fellowship was the best thing that had happened to the prisons, and that he knew that many chaplains worked happily with us, but that there were still some who didn't. And he would like to know from those who didn't, why they didn't.

Also in 1988 Michael made a speech in Parliament during a Home Office debate on prisons. Furnished with material by the Chaplain-General, he spoke on behalf of the chaplaincy. And in that year the Bishop to Prisons invited me on to the Chaplain-General's Advisory Group. Also, our then Director, Peter Chadwick, and I were invited by the Chaplain-General to come to the whole of the chaplains' conference as their guests. Chaplains (the official church representatives) and volunteers (the lay people) were beginning to weld together to make a stronger body of Christ in the prisons.

A sea change had happened in the body of Christ in the prisons. But it had taken ten years before this started to show.

Then a marvellous thing happened in the 1990s. The Alpha courses began at Holy Trinity Church, Brompton, and were spreading to other churches. Prison Fellowship staff went to the training days and, with our volunteers, started doing Alpha courses in a few of the prisons.

Alpha in prisons really took off in 1995 when a team from Holy Trinity, Brompton, led by Emmy Wilson, went to Exeter Prison. Since then, a special prison Alpha department, led by Paul Cowley, has been put in place at Holy Trinity, Brompton, and, in the year 2000, there were Alpha courses in nearly all our prisons, encouraged and supported by the present Chaplain-General (again appointed from outside the prison service). Of course, nobody can do an Alpha course in a prison without the full co-operation of the chaplain, and in many cases the chaplains have emerged, and are emerging, as excellent Alpha team leaders.

In the mid-1980s the chaplains were declining in numbers. But now they are needed more than ever because the numbers of prisoners who are coming to faith in Christ in prison, and consequently the number in the chaplaincy groups, have both greatly increased. Several assistant chaplains, many of them lay people from our Prison Fellowship groups, have been appointed. And Prison Fellowship is working with the chaplaincy in providing specific programmes, for example – the Life Management Programmes that are jointly implemented through the chaplains, our staff and volunteers.

All this is a result of the grace of God and his wonderful love and kindness, and in answer to prayers from his people over many years, so that his will may be done on earth, as it is in heaven.

15 APAC PRISONS

Early in the life of Prison Fellowship in England and Wales, perhaps in 1982, we were offered a prison that had been closed down. Peter Timms, our then Director; Anthony Cordle, then a trustee, and I, drove to Shropshire and found this prison, miles away in some fields, empty except for a custodian who greeted us and let us in to explore to our hearts' content. We walked all round it, through it, and discussed and prayed. What could we do with it if we accepted this offer? We knew that we could run seminars based on Christian teaching, but apart from that we couldn't really think what we could do with it or in it that would be different from any other prison. Apart from Peter Timms, who had been a prison governor, we had very few people amongst our volunteers with the gifts and skills to run a prison, and we had no money. So very regretfully we decided to say thank you, but no, we couldn't use it.

However, as we walked back towards the car, the thought was impressed upon me that the time was coming when there would be a prison run on a Christian basis in England, and that I would recognise it when I saw it, but the time was not yet.

This recognition came five years later, in 1987. I was at a Prison Fellowship International Board meeting when Javier Bustamante, the South American Director of Prison Fellowship International told us of a prison in Brazil where the prisoners themselves ran the prison. Inmates were trusted to be keyholders and each inmate had a godparent in the community who looked after him and also kept in touch with his family. Each day they had prayer and bible study and, later in their sentence, they were allowed to work in the community before being released, so that they were prepared for life outside.

As I listened, I got more and more excited. This was what the Holy Spirit had impressed on me five years earlier. I knew that when the time was ripe we would have such a prison in England but God had impressed on us that he wanted the whole body of Christ throughout the country to be working together, and it was not yet ready for this step.

In 1988 the founders of this APAC prison (the Association for the Protection and Assistance of the Convicted) established Prison Fellowship Brazil, and at the 1992 Convocation in Seoul, South Korea, news of it was given to all the assembled delegations.

In 1993 Angus Creighton, Senior Social Worker in the Scottish Prison Service, a founder of Prison Fellowship Scotland and a valued colleague on the International Board, won a Winston Churchill Memorial Trust Travelling Fellowship. This enabled him to spend six weeks in the APAC prison in Brazil, making a study of how it worked. He kindly sent me a copy, and again the excitement rose in me. This was surely God's idea for prisons. Each of our trustees had a copy, and we noted that in God's timing this would come about in England and Wales.

In 1995 things started to come together, and by the end of that year we had set up a little APAC subgroup of our Prison Fellowship trustees and staff. We invited on to it the Assistant Chaplain-General at the Home Office, who came representing the chaplaincy. Our brief was to pray and think about how we might proceed.

Prison Fellowship in Scotland had been asked by the then Director of the Scottish Prison Service, Alan Walker, to try to set up an APAC prison in Scotland. He sent a prison governor to the prison in Brazil, and with Angus Creighton they worked on a plan. Unfortunately, at that time they were not able to proceed. Prison Fellowship Scotland later rang us to report that Alan Walker had been moved to England where he had a job as Director of Prisons, South.

So in 1996 we met Alan Walker and he was thrilled to discover that we were working on a plan for an APAC prison. We told him that for such a prison to succeed, we needed it to be a local prison so that inmates could be reintegrated with their families and communities and we could link them up with volunteers from the local churches to help them with jobs, etc. He generously offered us a member of his staff to do research for us, and she came up with a list of suitable prisons.

Also that year, an excellent documentary film about the Brazilian APAC project, made by Penelope Lee and called 'Love is not a luxury', was made available to us. At last interested people were able to see exactly what the Brazilian prison looked like, and how it differed from any other prison in the world.

As I was praying about our little APAC subgroup, I had the impression of a three-legged milking stool. The seat of this stool was the prison, and the three legs were the volunteers, the prison administration and the justice system. Prison Fellowship had trained volunteers to work in prison; we saw Alan Walker and his assistant as the prison administration; and now we needed the third leg.

Many years ago Prison Fellowship International had teamed up with Justice Fellowship, started by Dan Van Ness in the United States, to look into biblical concepts of justice, and our present Director in England, Peter Walker, had become very interested in what they were doing. We thought we should have such a body here that brought together people of different professions.

After one of our APAC subgroup meetings I was in church

and praying about how we could find our justice 'leg' for the stool. As I rose from prayer, there was a man standing behind me who tapped me on the shoulder. He said that he was very impressed with our Prison Fellowship newsletter, and wondered if there was anything he could do to help. He was a member of our congregation and I knew him by sight, but I didn't know who he was. I asked him what he did.

'I'm a judge,' he said.

Since that time Judge Christopher Compston has been on our APAC subgroup.

Chuck Colson was planning to come to England in June 1996 to speak at a dinner for lawyers and he made himself available to Prison Fellowship for the afternoon. We jumped at this opportunity and wrote to Christians from amongst lawyers, policemen and probation officers, and also other people who were interested, including the Chaplain-General of Prisons and the Prison Ombudsman, Sir Peter Woodhead, inviting them to tea in the House of Lords. It was to be hosted by the Marquess of Reading, then a trustee, and would be chaired by Christopher Compston. From that tea came the inception of the Christian Justice Alliance.

All this was in the lead-up to a conference we were planning for December 1996.

We held this conference, organised with the encouragement of the Prison Service, in Church House, Westminster. To it we invited Christian prison governors, chaplains and volunteers, and people involved in the justice system and grant-making trusts.

It was a most exciting day. Ron Nikkel, President of Prison Fellowship International, gave a keynote address, telling us, amongst other things, about the APAC prison in Ecuador, which had opened in 1994 after two years' preparation, having been inspired by the Brazilian model. We heard from our Scottish brethren, and others, about what they had learned from their visits to the Brazilian prison. And we heard about the Cursillo weekend, which is used every six months in the prison in Brazil.

Cursillo (or 'a short little course') is a wonderful experience. It had been devised in Spain as a short course in Christian teaching for the purpose of revitalising the church after the Civil War in the 1930s, and had spread to other countries. The founders of the Brazilian prison had been involved in Cursillo in their local churches and from this background had come together to teach it in the prison. Originally a Catholic course, it has now spread to other denominations, and in England is in use in Catholic and Anglican dioceses. Several of our trustees and staff have done their Cursillo and early in 1996 had come together with other Cursillistas to do the first Tres Dias weekend (the inter-denominational name of the Cursillo), which had been led by one of our area co-ordinators, Marian Cotterill. To this came three of the Prison Fellowship Scotland Trustees and several of our volunteers, to prepare us for doing this course in prison. Before then, a Cursillo had been done only once in an English prison, by the chaplaincy team, and it had been a very moving experience for everyone.

My husband, Michael, chaired the conference in Church House at which we were told all these things, and all our trustees and APAC subgroup members chaired the group discussions that took place in the afternoon, reporting back at the end of the day.

Dan Van Ness, now on the staff team of Prison Fellowship International, was there to encourage our fledgling Justice Fellowship group, and Fritz Block from Switzerland, on the International Board representing Europe, was also there. We all went away invigorated and encouraged by the day.

Then in 1997 two things happened. In March that year a 'Kairos' wing was opened in the Verne Prison in Dorset. And the Prison Alpha Course, which had started in 1995, was taken into many more prisons.

The Kairos course is an eighteen-week course devised some years ago in North America specifically to be run in prisons. It includes the Cursillo weekend, with added weeks of further teaching, and is run by trained volunteers from local churches who commit themselves to going into the prison for each of the eighteen weeks. A new team is taken into a prison every six months, though not necessarily with the same volunteers.

In England, there was some confusion at first because, by a misunderstanding, the original Trust set up to raise funds for Kairos in prisons was called the Kairos-APAC Trust. Consequently, many people, including some from the prison administration who had come to our APAC conference, thought Prison Fellowship had been involved in setting it up. In fact, we had not. It was set up by local initiative on the part of some individuals and staff at the Verne Prison. Since its inception, however, many Prison Fellowship volunteers have been involved in visiting the Verne Prison and in delivering programmes. Fortunately this misunderstanding has been cleared up. The Kairos-APAC Trust came to an end, and it is now simply called the Kainos Trust, meaning 'a new thing' (a modest name change decided on by its new Trustees) and with the earlier reference to APAC deleted. There are now three Kainos wings in three different prisons, one for women and two for men.

This Kainos initiative is proving a wonderful experiment. It enables inmates, both men and women, who are committed to wanting to change, to live for six months in a designated wing of the prison run by dedicated Christian volunteers. It is marvellous to see the difference in their behaviour and attitudes when they are treated with the dignity that is integral to the Christian world view that we are made in the image of God.

Also in 1997 we invited Emmy Wilson, leader of the HTB
(Holy Trinity, Brompton) Prison Alpha Team, to join us on
our APAC subgroup. For several years we had been seeking
ways to involve local churches in the ministry of welcoming
ex-offenders and their families on and prior to their release.
Through one of our trustees, who was Chairman of the Bible
Society, we had prepared a book for churches on the subject
of prison ministry. Now the growth of Alpha throughout
churches of all denominations, and in the prisons, gave us a
way of drawing in the churches. So we invited Emmy on to
our thinking and praying team.

In 1999 the fruit of this co-operation came in the first
national prison Alpha conference, beautifully hosted by
Holy Trinity, Brompton. The speakers were Sandy Millar and
Nicky Gumbel, the Chaplain-General of Prisons, the Prison
Ombudsman, and the Bishop of Kensington. Emmy Wilson
and Paul Cowley (head of the Prison Alpha Department at
HTB) also spoke, and so did several ex-prisoners. In the
afternoon Peter Walker and our staff team undertook
training for the volunteers.

The foundations of God's house had to be laid in prayer.
And God had said that he wanted the whole body of Christ,
working together, to build his house from the ground floor
up. This was now happening. Many new volunteers were
coming in through the Alpha courses and through the
dioceses that ran Tres Dias and Cursillos – those doing their
Cursillos could help with weekends in the relevant wings.

A scripture that had come very much to mind as we
prayed throughout 1997 was, 'How good and pleasant it is
when brothers dwell together in unity . . . For there the
LORD has commanded his blessing' (Psalm 133:1, 3, RSV). So
that year we invited two trustees from Kainos, John Broadley
and Ian Aldred, to join us. Our common brief was – and still
is – to share information and to pray for one another and for

all the various roles and functions in which we were involved in the prisons so that the body of Christ might be united as we worked together.

In 1998 Prison Fellowship was asked by the Prison Service to do some research into the amount of time that was needed on a course before a real change of lifestyle, attitude and behaviour could be established. Our research concluded that eighteen to twenty-four months were needed. We showed our proposals to the then Director of the Prison Service, Richard Tilt, who was very supportive and enthusiastic about the possibilities, but then retired from the prison service on health grounds.

In July 1999 Prison Fellowship International invited representatives from ten countries to an APAC summit meeting in Quito, Ecuador. By then five of these countries – Brazil, Ecuador, Peru, Argentina and the USA (where APAC is called InnerChange) – already had APAC prisons. The other five countries – Prison Fellowship New Zealand, Norway, South Africa, Scotland, and England and Wales – were working to implement APAC. The meeting was chaired by Dan Van Ness, and the delegation included two of the 'founding fathers' Mario Ottoboni (Brazil) and Dr Jorge Crespo (Ecuador).

Peter Walker, our Prison Fellowship Director, was our English representative, and he came back full of enthusiasm, thoroughly energised by the two-week trip, which had taken in the two prisons in Ecuador, and the American InnerChange prison in Texas. On his return he wrote an excellent report which we have been able to show to relevant people.

Then in 2000 our Prison Fellowship Chairman, Lady Georgie Wates, took a special interest group, including the Chaplain-General of Prisons, and a prison governor, to Houston, Texas InnerChange prison, which is now being run in Iowa, as well as Texas.

A scripture that has been much in my mind while praying over the change going on in people in the APAC prisons is Mark 2:22, where Jesus says: 'No-one pours new wine into old wineskins. If he does, the wine will burst the skins, and both the wine and the wineskins will be ruined. No, he pours new wine into new wineskins.' (The note in the margin of the NIV says: 'In ancient times goatskins were used to hold wine. As the fresh grape juice fermented, the wine would expand and the new wineskin would stretch. But a used skin, already stretched, would break. Jesus brings a newness that cannot be confined within the old forms.')

Prisoners are turning to Christ in great numbers through the Alpha courses, and the growing and strengthening of the body of Christ, and this new life of Christ needs new forms of prison regimes to help disciple men and women who want to be changed into his likeness. This new training for life is being done in the APAC prisons. In these prisons the recidivism rate is below 16 per cent, and sometimes below 5 per cent, whereas in other prisons the rate is from 75 to 85 per cent, and some people are in and out of prison all their lives.

I believe the Lord would like his body to set up APAC prisons throughout the world: the body of Christ building the house, the prisons being part of the ground floor.

'He will not falter or be discouraged till he establishes justice on earth' (Isa. 42:4, NIV).

16 TRACING THE THREADS

On 2 October 1998 I went to the Methodist Central Hall, Westminster, for a service of thanksgiving for the life of the Revd Dr Donald English. I was very sad. A couple of years before this event my mind had started going back, over and over again, to the period of the Nationwide Initiative in Evangelism, and its executive committee, which had sat from March 1978 till July 1981. I had been a member of this committee, which had organised the Nottingham Assembly in 1980. Sixteen years later I would wake in the early hours of the morning and find myself remembering conversations and issues discussed during those meetings, under Donald's chairmanship, which I had not thought of over all those years.

From time to time, I had bumped into Donald, and his wife Bertha, but only fleetingly, the last time being when they were leading the One Voice Mission in York in 1992 and were staying in the house next to ours in York, and, as we were mostly in London, had borrowed our garage. Recently I had begun to think that I would love to talk to Donald and find out what had happened to the 'One Body' baby that had been born at the Nottingham Assembly in September 1980. Now I had left it too late.

At the service of thanksgiving, I sat, very sad, in a hall full of very sad people, many of them weeping openly. But I was totally galvanised by the platform party. Cardinal Hume was there, and said one of the prayers. An Orthodox priest was there. There were tributes from Dr Frances Alguire, President of the World Methodist Council, from Billy Graham and Cardinal Cassidy – who were not present

(Billy's voice came over on a tape!). So many different denominations were represented on the platform. The Revd Dr Peter Graves, Superintendent Minister of Westminster Central Hall, said, as he welcomed us to the service, 'Donald often used to say: "We don't need more arguments for the gospel. We need more free samples – people who, by their life and witness, radiate the joy and power of faith." Donald was such a witness and we thank God for him.'

The Revd Martin Broadbent thanked God, amongst other things, for Donald's 'visionary leadership'. The Archbishop of Canterbury, represented by the Bishop of Lambeth, remembered Donald's commitment to inter-church co-operation, especially through the Free Church Council and the World Methodist Council, and prayed for the unity of the church, asking God that the spiritual unity which was already ours as believers in the one Lord and members of the one body might, by God's grace, increasingly become a visible unity so that God's church in every place 'may demonstrate the healing and reconciling power of the gospel'. And there was a most moving sermon by Donald's friend, the Revd Brian Hoare, former President of the Methodist Conference, about Donald the man and based on Colossians 3:12-17.

As I watched and listened, I thought, 'Wow! It looks as if Donald embodied in himself all that NIE was about!'

Then in January 2000 Michael and I went to another wonderful service in the Methodist Central Hall, Westminster. This was Capital Joy 2000, organised by Churches Together in England, the ecumenical organisation which includes the Roman Catholic Church and most of the country's Christian bodies, and presented as brought to us by the London Church Leaders: 'a gathering of Christian Church Leaders from the thirty-three Boroughs of London, working together to co-ordinate the Churches' presence and voice'.

The service was quite outstanding. The Wood Green Gospel Choir and Band had us all singing, and dancing as we sang. The compère was delightful and beautifully brought in all the different speakers, readers and prayers, who were of all denominations and churchmanships. The lessons were read by the MP Paul Boateng, representing the Government, Baroness Scotland of Asthal, representing the House of Lords, Margery Barrow, representing the Black churches, and the Rt Revd Dr John Sentamu, representing the London Church Leaders. The address was given by the Archbishop of Canterbury, Dr George Carey, who spoke in a delightful, all-inclusive manner.

Also present were Roman Catholic clergy from Westminster Cathedral, and mayors, members of Parliament and civic dignitaries. But what galvanised me most was the discovery that until his death the previous year, Cardinal Basil Hume had himself been Chairman of the London Church Leaders, and had been particularly enthusiastic at the prospect of this evening of prayer and praise in the Methodist Central Hall. 'It will be great fun,' he had said.

What had particularly stunned me was that earlier, in the build-up to the setting up of the Nationwide Initiative in Evangelism, the 'Roman Catholic Hierarchy had informed us that it was not able to become a constituent member of NIE, though it continued to recommend positive co-operation in the NIE programme at local level where this was possible and two Roman Catholics, Canon Dennis Corbishley and Sister Kira Soldhoost, were appointed to the NIE committee as consultants!' There had been much sadness amongst us that the Roman Catholics were being so standoffish. Yet now Cardinal Hume had not only been actively involved but had chaired the setting up of this whole service. What had happened in the last twenty years to bring about this change of heart and wonderful unity?

In October 1980, the month after the Nottingham Assembly, I had asked if I could do the devotions at the Initiative Prayer Meeting. At that time, in our little Monday intercession group meeting (which has now been going each week for over thirty years) we had been rejoicing over the birth of the 'One Body' baby, and the Lord had impressed on me that he would like me to tell the story of the birth (which I have recounted in chapter 9 of this book) to the NIE committee. So I asked him: 'Now the baby is born, Lord, how about the work of the Nationwide Initiative on Evangelism? Where do we go from here?' And he gave us two pictures, which I went on to share with the committee members.

The first picture was of a stork! bringing a baby and laying it down by the banks of a river. The accompanying thought was that you cannot leave a newborn baby on its own to fend for itself because if you do, it will die. It needs to be looked after until it can look after itself. A baby needs a family.

And as I shared this, I found myself saying: 'And Satan hates this baby and will do his best to get rid of it. And as Miriam and her mother and the princess looked after Moses when Pharaoh had all the Hebrew boys killed, and as Joseph and Mary looked after Jesus when Herod had all the other babies killed, so the enemy will do his utmost to get rid of this Baby and so we need a family to look after him.

The second picture was of a large piece of ground divided into allotments. In some allotments, fruit and flowers were growing, in others, there were vegetables, and some had a mixture of flowers, fruit and vegetables. In each, a man was working away, tending his plants. Then there was a sense of each of these men leaning on the fence, having a chat with his neighbour and making comments, such as, 'What lovely marrows you've got! I don't know anything about marrows, I only know about peas and beans. Please tell me about your marrows and I'll tell you about my peas and beans.'

At the same time as this picture was given in the intercession group, the interpretation was also given. It was about clergy fraternals, with a sense of clergy of different denominations and churchmanships coming together in particular geographical areas for friendship and fellowship, worshipping the Lord together, sharing their concerns for the locality, and praying for each other. These were the sorts of places where people could be encouraged to get together and admire one another's vegetables!

Twenty years later, after this glorious service, Capital Joy 2000, I was determined to follow the threads from the birth of the 'One Body' baby in 1980 to the wonderful Churches Together celebrations that had taken place over the millennium period.

The first thread I tried to follow was in response to the question: What happened to the 'family' looking after this 'One Body' baby? Did such a family come into being? I had envisaged a family of three or four clergy of different denominations working together in a core group, as a visual aid of the unity of the body of Christ.

In September 1981, after I had left, and the Initiative Committee had given way to the Initiative Council, I had received a letter from Donald English, thanking me for being on the Committee and for giving 'those marvellous pictures in words you painted for us at various meetings'. He wrote, 'You will be interested to know that the first meeting of the Council moved a considerable way towards the possibility of a smaller group to think and pray together. I think you may feel you have had that idea before! The wonderful thing was that it didn't come from any of the previous members of the Committee. I had a feeling somebody was praying somewhere!'

Who had been in this core group? What had they come up with? During the course of 2000, I got in touch with Gavin

Reid (the Anglican bishop of Maidstone), the Revd Tom Houston, Dr Martin Conway, the Revd. Roger Whitehead, and Roger Forster, all of whom had been on the Initiative Committee, and they pointed me in the right direction to find clues.

Tom referred me to a book by Roger Whitehead, published in 1990 and called *An Unwanted Child? The story of NIE*. This is a mine of information, starting with the setting up of the Lambeth Group in 1976 under the chairmanship of Donald Coggan, the Archbishop of Canterbury, and taking us through the discussions on the NIE Committee, the Nottingham Assembly itself, and events afterwards. It ends with a conclusion by the Revd Canon Martin Reardon, then General Secretary of Churches Together in England, which, of course, didn't exist in 1980.

This 1990 publication describes a frustrating, confusing scenario, with lots of misunderstandings between different groups and churches, and seemingly nothing conclusive at the end. But clearly something did come out of it, as Capital Joy 2000 so vividly showed. Roger Whitehead writes:

> *One of the features of the Assembly was the widespread recognition of Donald English as a national church leader. Colin Buchanan perceived this and during the worship on the last morning he 'commissioned' Donald by prayer specifically to continue his work within and for NIE, an act which subsequently had considerable personal significance for Donald and sustained him during the trying days ahead. It had become clear that if the first phase of NIE had been the tale of one Donald (Coggan), the next stage would be of another Donald. In every subsequent change to the shape of the Initiative, there was never any doubt that everyone wanted Donald English to continue to lead it.*

Roger Whitehead, *A Unwanted Child?* page 42

In what did the 'visionary leadership' that had been
mentioned at the thanksgiving service for Donald's life
consist? Donald had just been appointed General Secretary
of the Methodist Church Home Mission Division, and the
Methodist Church would not release him from his role there
to be leader of the NIE, but 'did allow and encourage him to
remain chairman of the Initiative and play a full part in its
development and the work related to that'. Donald always
refused to be a leader on his own, but said he wanted to work
with a small group.

In his chapter on preparing for the Nottingham Assembly,
Roger Whitehead wrote of the devotions at each of the
Committee meetings, which were led each time by a different
person. I was surprised the find the following comment:

*Sylvia Mary Alison shared her visions for NIE which were often in
the form of pictures. As Donald English remarked, 'We remembered
them clearly and could refer back to them months later when all the
other talking had long since been forgotten.' One, for example, was of
three or four people in the capsule of a spaceship, and was understood
to be three or four members called to meet together frequently to
discern God's agenda for the Committee.*

An Unwanted Child?

I had forgotten this picture of a capsule. It had presented
itself to my mind during the first Council of Reference
meeting after the Assembly, a meeting which had been
chaired by the Archbishop of York, Dr Stuart Blanch, and I
had shared it with the members. In essence, of course, the
idea behind the picture was similar to that of the 'family'
looking after the baby: the people in the capsule were the
clergy of different denominations. But it was different in that
the spaceship was flying off. Pondering the significance of
this now, I see this capsule as the new little shoot coming out
of the stump that I wrote about in chapter 9: the body of

Christ life coming away from the carnal structures. No wonder there had been so much confusion at the time amongst people wedded to the old structures!

Back to Donald's leadership. While he was leading the Methodist Home Mission Division, he started the Home Mission Group, bringing together the Secretaries of the Home Mission Divisions of different denominations. They meet once a quarter, and there are always three, four or five who come. These are not the headline church leaders, but they are very important for the working together of different denominations, and were pivotal for the Decade of Evangelism starting in 1990. Brian Hoare wrote:

> When the British Council of Churches Evangelism committee took over NIE's work, Donald was seen as the only person who could carry the confidence and support of others (particularly the evangelical constituency) into the new structures. Similarly when the British Council of Churches gave way to Churches Together in England, Donald was asked to chair the Churches Together Co-ordinating group for Evangelisation.

Brian Hoare, PROFILE – Donald English

In 1990 Donald asked Roger Whitehead to be the Executive Secretary of the Churches Co-ordinating Group for Evangelisation of Churches Together in England, a post which Roger still holds.

As I continued to trace the part played by Donald English, a very large present was handed to me by the Revd Brian Hoare in the form of papers relating to the One Voice Mission in York led by Donald in 1992. This was when I had last seen him. Although we had not been to any of the meetings, we had heard that this mission was making a remarkable impact on York. Three hundred churches worked together, Donald having personally met each of the clergy, of all the denominations.

The evening meetings were all held in the Barbican, a secular meeting place in York city centre. Donald gave the address every evening, and spoke every lunchtime in a different church of a different denomination. The evening meetings were very varied, with mime artists, choirs, dancers, theatre groups, interviews – all thought-provoking and designed to make people think.

The final celebration was in York Minster, the Anglican cathedral, with the Archbishop of York, John Habgood, who had given his testimony during one of the Barbican meetings. Again Donald gave the address. But the thing that gave me the most pleasure was the discovery that the event was organised by three chairmen: Fr Cyril Brooks (Roman Catholic), the Revd David Mullins (Methodist), and Canon John Young (Anglican). They had to sit down together and work things out between them and then come out with 'one voice'. (The Revd David Mullins told me that Donald was very humble, and although he was the leader, he said to them that he was there to do as they told him.)

And the money flowed in, and the people came. 'How good and pleasant it is when brothers dwell in unity . . . For there the LORD has commanded the blessing, life for evermore' (Psalm 133:1, 3, RSV).

It seemed to me that this event beautifully fleshed out the picture of the piece of ground divided into allotments in which different people worked their patch, but then came together to admire one another's vegetables!

Now how about Cardinal Hume? And when did the Roman Catholic Church become fully involved? The answer was given to me by Martin Conway, who wrote to me saying:

> *The story I told you came from the Swanwick conference on the future of the 'ecumenical instruments' of the British and Irish Churches, held in September 1987. Its purpose was to bring together the findings of the four conferences held earlier that year in England,*

*Scotland, Wales and Ireland, in which the churches who had
participated in the Lent 1986 programme (with the study book* What
on Earth is the Church for? *by Martin Reardon) could reflect
together on the appropriate shape of the ecumenical instruments
(local, regional and national) for the years ahead. In this the Roman
Catholic Church had agreed to play a full part, so that many of us
were hoping that this could be the time – at last! – when they would
be ready to actually join the National Council of Churches. So the
constituency of the meeting was largely the officially appointed
representatives of the Churches, along with staff of the British Council
of Churches (which had said it was ready to 'die in order to be reborn')
and a small number of people appointed by those 'ecumenical
agencies' which had an 'observer status' with the old British Council
of Churches.*

Martin Conway continues:

*This national conference at Swanwick was not without its moments
of frustration, partly because at various points the Roman Catholic
representatives still seemed insistent on keeping their distance from
those from the other Churches. This was particularly true at a Mass
which Cardinal Basil Hume celebrated for the conference as a whole
but at which only Roman Catholics were allowed to receive the bread
and wine. In a small discussion group later that day (one of many into
which the conference was divided for one session each day) questions
were put to the Cardinal as to why his Church felt unable to let the rest
of us participate fully. He was courteous enough to explain at some
length just why they stuck to this policy. When he finished there was
an awkward silence, broken when the group's chairman, a senior
minister of the United Reformed Church, said: 'Do you realise,
Cardinal, that sounds to most of us as if your Church doesn't really
think we are Christians?' At which there was an even longer silence,
broken when Basil Hume said quietly: 'I am so grateful that you dared
to say that to me; I have never had it said to me before, but as I hear
you now, you are helping me to see the truth in it.' Within 24 hours,*

*after further meetings with his fellow Catholic delegates, he announced
to the conference, to huge applause, that the Roman Catholic Church
of England and Wales was now ready to work with the other Churches
towards a 'new' national Council of Churches in which they would be
members with those others.*

*As a result of that conference the four new national bodies,
Churches Together in England being the one for England, were
formed, with what is now called 'Churches Together in Britain and
Ireland' serving as the overall body for the total Christian community
in these islands. The old British Council of Churches happily died to
make way for these new 'ecumenical instruments' in all of which the
Roman Catholic Church takes a full part.*

This transition is fully written up in a booklet called *The
Next Step for Churches Together in Pilgrimage*, published in 1989.
From this booklet I quote two paragraphs, under the
heading Aims and Functions:

*The aims and functions of Churches Together in England have
been developed and adapted from those in the Swanwick Report and
are as follows: To be a visible sign of the Churches' commitment to
one another, in obedience to Our Lord's Prayer 'that all of them may
be one, Father, just as you are in me and I in you; may they also be in
me so that the world may believe that you have sent me' (John 17:21,
NIV).*

*To encourage the review of ecclesiastical boundaries in England so
that they may be aligned as closely as possible with each other and
with the civil boundaries in order to promote the shared mission of
the churches.*

The Next Step for Churches Together in Pilgrimage

In the Catholic weekly publication, *The Tablet*, dated 16
September 2000, there was a little article headed 'Evangelists
share insights' which grabbed my full attention. The article
said:

John Paul II in the 1980s called 1991-2000 to be the 'decade of evangelism'. The initiative was discussed and agreed by all the major Christian denominations. In 1989 the Lambeth Conference called on the Anglican Communion to move from a culture of maintenance to a culture of mission.

This last sentence struck me particularly because in the 1970s, in the run-up to the 1978 Lambeth conference – the regular ten-yearly gathering of Anglican bishops world-wide – we had been praying for the bishops in our Monday intercession group. And as we prayed we received a picture of a catafalque. (My dictionary describes this as: 'a decorated platform on which the coffin of a distinguished person stands during the funeral, or while the remains are lying in state'.) At each corner of this coffin, or very ornate stone tomb, there was a man standing still, his head lowered, guarding it. As we pondered this picture and prayed for understanding, we had the impression of the Church of England's bishops being guardians of the tomb of the dead Christ. There seemed to be no sense that he was risen and alive, walking the streets of England.

Apparently, at the Lambeth Conference of 1988 the Anglican Communion had discussed the Pope's initiative and agreed it. That's why *The Tablet* announced: 'In 1989 the Lambeth Conference called on the Anglican Communion to move from a culture of maintenance to a culture of mission.'[1]!

And what a lot has happened in the last ten years! The Alpha courses, which have now taken off round the world, started in Holy Trinity, Brompton, with Charles Marnham, who was a curate there in 1977-79. Alpha was further developed by another curate, John Irvine, in the '80s, and

[1] See Appendix 4 for the full article

became the tool it has now become through Nicky Gumbel in the '90s. It is used throughout the British Isles by all the different denominations, and in nearly all the prisons, bringing many to new life in Christ.

In 2000 I had a lovely afternoon with Roger Forster, who started the Ichthus Christian Fellowship in 1974. The work of Ichthus is described in the literature Roger gave me:

> *We began with a mandate from God to evangelise London and the nations by planting churches of Christ – exalting, Bible-loving believers committed to the Lord Jesus Christ, to his mission and to one another. By 1982 we had grown from 14 people to around 400 and 2 new congregations were being planted. Since then some 27 congregations have been established right across south-east London, reaching into south-west and central London, Essex and Kent, and a further 130 churches in the UK and Europe are linked with us. We also have a large and thriving overseas missions movement with 80 missionaries working in 25 nations, with a special focus on the least evangelised nations of the world.*

> *'March for Jesus' has spread throughout the world and is one of the most major Christian initiatives to come out of the UK for a long time. Without the contribution of Lynn Green (YWAM), Gerald Coates and Graham Kendrick, 'March for Jesus' would never have got to where it is today, but it is a privilege to remember how we began these marches in a small way every time we sought to plant a congregation in south-east London. It has now gone global and millions more are yet to take their stance in marching for Jesus around the earth.*

Roger Forster was, of course, a member of the NIE Committee, and Ichthus is part of Churches Together in England, bringing in mostly Pentecostals and Charismatics.

There is a lovely photograph in *Livelink*, the Ichthus magazine, of the Archbishop, George Carey, and his wife Eileen marching and singing with Roger Forster, Gerald

Coates and others, in June 2000, in Greenwich, home of Greenwich Mean Time. This was to celebrate the millennium, and it was the final (official) 'March for Jesus' in Great Britain (called Jesus Day). Roger writes:

> As we close the chapter on the official organisation called 'March for Jesus', first we must say that 'March for Jesus' is not over, it has just begun with around 15 million people taking part globally. Now it is over to you, that is, you have been on marches, you know how to do it, so keep marching as God leads . . . What has been its significance? Unity, evangelism, being counted for God, coming out into the streets like Jesus, taking the walls off our churches, praise, worship and intercession etc.,. But the major thing I want to emphasise is . . . that God is a God who is on the move!

I was fascinated to learn that 2000 was the last 'official' 'March for Jesus'. As I started this chapter I had the sense that this 'One Body' baby, born in 1980, was, in the year 2000, twenty years old and therefore an adult. Now here Roger seems to be saying, 'Now you are all grown up, you can do your own marching, as God leads.'

So we have started the new millennium with this little shoot that sprang out of the stump of the tree becoming a sapling – no longer a baby, but a young adult – the life of Christ in all the Churches working together, marching throughout the land.

I close this chapter with the article from *The Tablet*, dated 16 September 2000.

EVANGELISTS SHARE INSIGHTS

Churches Together in England, the ecumenical organisation which includes the Catholic Church and most of the country's Christian bodies, has issued a list of 20 insights learned from the "decade of evangelism".

Launching the document, called "20 from 10", the Anglican

Bishop of Maidstone, Gavin Reid, said the Churches "have had to put themselves back to school in a post-Christian, post-modern age." This had led the Churches to become more aware of their resources. "This is a chastening time", he said, "when there is interest in spirituality but it is not translated into people looking to the Church."

John Paul II in the 1980s called for 1991-2000 to be the "decade of evangelism". The initiative was discussed and agreed by all the major Christian denominations. In 1989 the Lambeth Conference called on the Anglican Communion to move from a culture of maintenance to a culture of mission.

Examples of the 20 insights discussed by "20 from 10" are: "Evangelism is more effective when ecumenical"; "Most people come to faith gradually" and "Good evangelism is an invitation, not a confrontation". They can be read at www.evangelism.uk.net.

The executive secretary of the Churches' Group for Evangelisation, the Revd Roger Whitehead, noted: "Doing evangelism together is what unites churches, whereas 20 years ago evangelism was what divided them".

ENDPIECE

In October 2000 we had our twenty-first anniversary thanksgiving service for Prison Fellowship England and Wales. It was a wonderful afternoon. We held the service at Holy Trinity, Brompton, and 500 of our volunteers came to it from all over the country. Many brought banners, beautifully made by their groups, representing the prisons they work and pray for.

Our trustees had started by hosting a celebration lunch in Church House for about a hundred special guests. They included former trustees and members of staff, special friends from Prison Alpha and the Kainos wings, donors and supporters from over the years. The European Director of Prison Fellowship International, Ivan Sotirov, and the Chairman of Prison Fellowship Norway, Ingvald Viken, also came. The Revd John Harris, our first administrator when we were launched in 1979, flew over from Florida to be with us, and shared with us, humorously and delightfully, some early memories. Then Peter Chadwick, our Director from 1985-1992, gave some more interesting reminiscences. He was followed by Richard Sewell, who was a volunteer from the very beginning, then a trustee, and treasurer – which he still is!

When we all went into the church, it was such a thrill to see all these faithful prison volunteers, several of whom had been prisoners themselves.

We had a wonderful service, led by Georgie Wates, our Chairman. I have the programme before me. Chuck Colson spoke on video, on the subject, 'In the beginning'. I spoke on 'first steps', and Ron Nikkel, President of Prison Fellowship

International, spoke on 'growing up'. We had worship and thanksgiving, and a Bible reading from Isaiah 42:1-9, read by Helen Durant, our longest-serving staff member. The Revd Tom Johns, Assistant Chaplain-General, led prayers of thanksgiving, and Peter Walker, our current Executive Director, talked on 'developing new strengths'.

One of our volunteers told us a wonderful story, with a video clip, about a young burglar who broke into her house. Even as he was robbing her, she told him that Jesus loved him, and she loved him. Several years later she met him in the prison she was visiting. He is now married, with a wife and child, and a job, and she is in close touch with the little family as his substitute mum.

In our Annual Report celebrating twenty-one years of prison ministry, we had messages from the Archbishop of Canterbury, the Home Secretary, Chuck Colson, Ron Nikkel, a prison governor, and the Chaplain-General of Prisons.

In my message I wrote:

In November 1978 at our first conference, when Chuck Colson came to tell us what Prison Fellowship in the USA was beginning to do, a baby was born. In March 1979, when Prison Fellowship England and Wales was officially launched, I spoke of the birth of this baby. I said that a baby was small, looked like a baby, and had no resemblance to the adult it would one day become. How it developed would depend on all of us, chaplains and volunteers – Christians working together in the world of prisons . . . Now this is the year 2000, and there is absolutely no knowing what this adult – the body of Christ in the prisons – will do in the years to come as we follow our Servant King.

APPENDIX 1

Letters to Sylvia Mary written by the At Revd Lord Runcie, former Archbishop of Canterbury, not long before he died.

March 2000

Such an enjoyable and encouraging lunch together merits more than a mere card; but I have been surrounded with correspondence as my secretary is skiing! But I have now read the book and the account of the Dartmouth mission by Michael Green. Both have been good for my health and morale and I appreciated enormously the story Sylvia Mary told about the spiritual fall out from our conversations in the eighties. I am proud to be part of the Prison Fellowship story…

Robert

May 2000

Dear Sylvia Mary

I am sorry to have sat on your text for so long; but I have not been in good health and dependent upon the prayers of the faithful for keeping me upright.

It all looks very promising and I certainly approve of your quotations from the Lambeth interview.

With love and prayers

APPENDIX 2

Reflections on a three-day mission in Dartmoor Prison by Canon Michael Green

Advisor in Evangelism to the
Archbishops of Canterbury and York

The background

A remarkable work of God is happening in our prisons. David Powe has seen more than a thousand inmates profess the Christian faith at Belmarsh in the last two years, and similar things are happening elsewhere.

Holy Trinity Brompton has been preeminent in this prison work. They have four full-time workers and an army of volunteers. They have arranged for Alpha courses in 123 of the 158 UK prisons, and more prisons are joining up all the time. Indeed, the work is now international. It is flourishing in the Texan prisons at the invitation of Governor George Bush: all thirty-five members of the first prison where it was tried became Christians. The work is taking off throughout South Africa's overcrowded jails, with their 154,000 inmates, as a result of a conference in Johannesburg last August.

At the triennial conference of the Prison Fellowship, held this year in Bulgaria, massive support was given for the use of Alpha in prisons world-wide. Since then Greece, Fiji, Kenya, Uganda, Poland, have come on board, and Norway is so thrilled with its impact that it is now in all their prisons. Clearly this is a remarkable situation.

The impact

The impact of these Alpha courses in changing attitudes and

behaviour is undeniable. In Dartmoor, for example, more than 300 of the 650 prisoners have professed faith and are showing the difference. I was privileged to meet the Governor, himself a non-practising Jew, and hear his commendation of the effectiveness of Alpha and the missions in his prison, and the changed attitudes of officers and inmates during the four years Alpha has been operating there. Sir Peter Woodhead, the Prison Ombudsman, recently declared his joy at hearing non-Christian governors and staffs say that they have noted a detectable increase in good behaviour among those claiming conversion. 'I have absolutely no doubt that Alpha has made a significant contribution to the reduction of crime in society.'

The Dartmoor missions

Three times a year Emmy Wilson and Paul Cowley (HTB full-time leaders) collect a team of fifteen to twenty volunteers and go to spend three very full days in the prison. They are now accompanied by a recent addition to the HTB staff, Charlotte Braithwaite, who is responsible for after-care when prisoners are released.

On December 20 I took three ordinands from Wycliffe Hall, Oxford, to share in this mission team of twenty (which came from no less than fourteen churches). The work is done in close co-operation with the superb chaplain, Bill Birdwood, who arranged accommodation in Christian homes nearby, and also hosted a relaxed reception for us one night.

We entered the prison shortly after 8.00 a.m. and left it about 5.30. The programme was repeated: once for the sex offenders (kept very separate in the prison) and once for the general prisoners. It was simple: a welcome as they were escorted in, extended praise, perhaps testimony from inmates, a substantial and challenging address, followed by personal ministry at the front, when all members of the team were engaged one-on-one.

The worship was sensitively led by Ali Berry, a gifted keyboard player (fresh from *The Phantom of the Opera* in London). Paul Cowley and Emmy Wilson were superb. It is unusual to see a woman like Emmy holding together such a tough operation with such distinction. Paul was once himself an inmate, which gives him great credibility: he is currently training part-time for Anglican ordination. T h e chapel was packed – the men had all volunteered to come. Dartmoor's chapel cannot accommodate more than seventy, and seventy there were.

The response

This was incredible. These tough men with blood on their hands were responding to Jesus Christ in a way I never see outside. On the second day they were itching to come forward and commit themselves to Christ before I had finished the talk. The response was not emotional but was intensely real.

On the first day a *double-lifer* was converted. He mentioned the agony he was suffering from his kidneys which had been getting unbearable recently. Emmy led him to Christ, laid her hand on his back, prayed for him, and the next day he came back to testify that the Lord had given him a good night's sleep and that his kidneys 'like a couple of great onions' were now fully 'sorted'. He was completely healed. This sort of thing makes an enormous impact in the prison.

A *sex offender* spoke of being delivered from the old habits after all types of secular therapy had failed.

A *man in a top bunk*, who knew nothing at all of Christianity, dreamed that he saw a man being hounded to his death by a cruel mob, and he tried in vain to restrain them. He saw this man being nailed to a cross and jerked into the ground, then knelt at his feet and said sorry for not having been any help. At once he felt blood from the cross immersing his head. He jumped out of the bunk and cried out. His cell mate happened to be a Christian and showed him the passion story, which was exactly what he had seen in his dream. This man is now one of the Christian leaders in the prison. Several of his family outside have been converted as a result.

John was the strong man of the prison. He had been a very violent masked robber and it had taken five officers to get him in. Nobody dared to cross him. Someone had once offered him a tract and he had thrust them up against the wall with a gun to their head! He is now another of the gentle Christian leaders in Dartmoor.

We saw, I suppose, more than thirty men make commitments to Christ with evident sincerity. They are going to need all the help they can get.

Problems

1. Upon release *the dangers of recidivism* are enormous. Many of these men have no family at all and only gang members to go back to. They are determined not to do this, and need immediate help on release. Charlotte's job at HTB involves providing these men with someone to meet them when they emerge, fixing up lively, understanding churches for them, and trying to get them accommodation and employment through the churches.

Though embryonic, this ministry will become absolutely crucial. It is something for bishops to urge their parishes to consider. This large number of Christian prisoners coming out must be cared for and could become the catalyst for renewal in many a congregation.

2. *The small size of the prison chapel* greatly hampers the work. The large Napoleonic chapel which could accommodate all

the inmates is derelict. The chaplain's vision (backed by the governor and some substantial donors) is to renovate it, and make an upstairs portion consisting of classrooms, etc., where visiting teachers can come in and given their services, building up Christian leaders among the Christian prisoners. Funds are urgently needed for this. If they come in, the job cold be done by next December.

3. *Proselytism* is theoretically banned, but prisoners do share their testimony boldly and invite others both to Alpha and to Christ. One man calls out promises from the Scriptures through his open window and this has affected some of his hearers! But fellowship is very restricted. Many of these men are 'banged up' in their cells for twenty-three hours a day. Yet they came into meetings radiant!

A good number can hardly read: learning scripture and choruses has been a great help. The work is now so extensive that there is a serious shortage of workers to follow up what has been achieved.

Conclusion
The mission was an incredible, life-changing privilege. Many ordinands should go on this!

APPENDIX 3
How the baby grew and developed

When the Nationwide Initiative in Evangelism closed in 1982, the British Council of Churches established an Evangelism Committee. For the first time in Britain, an ecumenical body put evangelism on its agenda. The Evangelism Committee continued until the British Council of Churches ceased in 1990 and each of the denominations took responsibility for evangelism. To take up the biblical picture and adapt it, you could say that a little child led the British Council of Churches into evangelism.

The 'ownership' of evangelism by the BCC and the sharing which had gone on in the committee meant that when the Lambeth Conference in 1988 called on the Communion to adopt the last decade of the twentieth century as 'a Decade of Evangelism' (echoing the Pope's call a year or two earlier for a Decade of Evangelisation), there was already in Church circles an acknowledgement that evangelism had to be shared. This, in parallel with the widespread inter-church support for initiatives like Mission England in the 1980s, created a climate in the Churches which made them receptive to the idea of a Decade of Evangelism. The little child had changed the way Churches looked at evangelism. In due course, that led Ichthus to become a member of CTE.

This new attitude led Donald English in 1988 to invite the other senior staff persons in each denomination with responsibility for evangelism to meet together two or three times a year for a couple of hours to share with each other. This was an informal occasion to keep in touch: but significantly no such regular meeting of staff persons in any area of church life had previously gathered in this way. It became a model commended to the other areas of church life (youth, social responsibility, etc.) when Churches Together in England was established in 1990. So it was natural, when Churches responded to the call for a Decade of Evangelism, for them to ask their 'decade officers' to meet together and work together. No major national initiative was launched by one Church alone during the Decade – they were all done corporately. The child had changed the way the Churches worked on evangelism.

When Churches Together in England was being formed the informal meeting of denominational evangelism staff persons became formal, and others were invited to join, reflecting the wide relationships which had been built up in NIE – indeed some of the NIE members became members of the new Group for Evangelisation – Donald English, Roger Forster and Gavin Reid were three. The membership of the Group was and is wider than that of CTE, including the New Churches, groups like the Brethren, the Evangelical Alliance and the Orthodox. The vision of evangelism being everyone's responsibility – the work of the whole Body of Christ – perceived in NIE became reality. The child had shared the vision.

There was another development of great significance. Bringing evangelism into the life of the Churches meant that it coalesced with other areas of church life and this emphasized the importance of the whole gospel to the whole person; the unhealthy division between 'evangelism' (seen as something personal) and 'Kingdom' (seen as social action) began to be eroded and this has continued throughout the 1990s.

There remain different emphases and arguments, but they now take place within the Church as part of its discernment rather than as battles between competing groups. The NIE sense of being held together under the compulsion of the Spirit has spread widely in the last twenty years.

Such developments have not taken place in any other part of the English-speaking world; but none of them had a Nationwide Initiative in Evangelism.

Revd Roger Whitehead